Tikkun Olam

Stories of Repairing an Unkind World

Marilyn Cohen Shapiro

Tikkun Olam: *Stories of Repairing an Unkind World*
Copyright © 2018 Marilyn Cohen Shapiro
All rights reserved.

Editor: Mia Crews

Cover Photos: Marilyn and Larry Shapiro visiting San Francisco. Pictures provided by Marilyn Cohen Shapiro. Background photo of the San Francisco Bridge from www.bigstockphoto.com

Cover by Mia Crews. Back cover photos provided by Marilyn Cohen Shapiro. Author photo by Skip Stowers.

Many of these stories first appeared in *The Jewish World* (http://jewishworldnews.org), *The Schenectady Daily Gazette* and *The Heritage Florida Jewish New* under the name Marilyn Shapiro. The author has tried to recreate events, locales and conversations from her memories of them to the best of her ability. Some of the names have been changed; real names are used with permission.

The author may be contacted via email at shapcomp18@gmail.com.
www.marilynshapiro.com

ISBN-13: 978-1722646974
ISBN-10: 1722646977

This book is dedicated
to my parents,
Francis and Bill Cohen

*"There are only two lasting bequests we can hope to give our children.
One of these is **roots**; the other, **wings**."*

Hodding Carter

Definitions of Jewish words

Bris: The Jewish birth ceremony during which a baby boy is brought into the Covenant of the Jewish people.

Dayanu: A song of gratitude sung toward the end of reading of the Haggadah, the book in which the story of the Exodus is recounted during the Passover Seder.

Haftorah: A series of selections from the book of Prophets. Read in synagogue as part of Jewish religious practice.

L'Shana Tova: "Have a good year!"

Mehitzah: A curtain which separates the men from the women in Orthodox synagogues.

Mitzvot: One of 613 commandments from Jewish Bible that relate to the religious and moral conduct of Jews.

Rosh Hashanah: The Jewish New Year. Usually falls in September or October.

Shabbos: Sabbath. Judaism's day of rest and seventh day of the week. Observed from sundown Friday to sundown Saturday.

Seder: A Jewish ritual feast that marks the beginning of the Jewish holiday of Passover.

Sh'ma: Prayer that serves as a centerpiece of the morning and evening Jewish prayer services.

Shiva: (Literally "seven") The week-long mourning period in Judaism for first-degree relatives.

Shul: Yiddish word for the synagogue.

Simcha: Celebration.

Tikkun Olam: The Jewish concept that suggests humanity's shared responsibility to heal, repair, and transform the world.

Torah: Judaism's most important text, containing the Five Books of Moses. It is the source of the Ten Commandments and the 613 mitzvot.

Tzedakah: Charity.

Yom Kippur: Day of Atonement. Annual Jewish observance of fasting, prayer and repentance. Considered the holiest day on the Jewish calendar.

Contents

Repairing the World	1
Holding On Tight	3
New Year, Old Traditions	7
I Can See Clearly Now	10
Who By Fire, Who By Water?	13
The Candle Debacle	16
Finding the Perfect Gift	19
"May the Force Be With You!"	22
Friends, Fried Rice, and Fortune Cookies	25
The Holiday Card	28
Disney Princesses and Purim Queens	31
Cutting It Close: The Passover Bris	34
Dayanu	37
The Goldene Medinah	40
The Four Cohen Kids	43
Pressing Question?	46
Eye of the Beholder	49
Don't Hoard the Charmin'	52
Today I Am A Woman!	55
The Simcha That Almost Wasn't	58
Generous Hearts	61
Never Forget	64
Golden Romances	67
Big Wheels and Big Hills	70
Bubbe Butt Paste	73
Adventures in Time Travel	76
The Shul at 10,200 Feet	79
Collect Memories, Not Things	82
If You Listen…	85
NOT the Party of the Century	88
"Let's RummiKub!"	91
Life Lessons From My Mom	94
Summertime and the Swimming Is Easy	97
Guess Who's Coming to Dinner	100

From Pizza Boy to Shuksuka Expert	103
Making the Best Out of Each Day	106
FLI's	109
Loveys	112
Her Own Best Advocate	115
Loving the Body I Have	119
Moving Mountains: Creating a Legacy	122
A Mensch of a Man	125
A Soldier, An Orphan, and a Photographer	129
Onto My Next Adventure	133
How I Came to Write a Book	136
Acknowledgements	139
About the Author	141

Repairing the World

Tikkun Olam, the Hebrew expression translated often as "repairing the world" is the Jewish moral principal that states every individual should leave this world better than he or she found it.

Melting glaciers and rising seas. The threat of nuclear war. The uptick of racist and xenophobic acts. Despite or maybe because of the current state of our world, it is more critical than ever for me to use my moral compass to point me in a direction that follows my values and helps create change for the better for others.

Until recently, I did not consider myself an activist. I was—admittedly—marginally involved in the Vietnam War protests and the 1972 Equal Rights Amendment fight. Although I have voted in almost every local, state, and national election, I have minimally involved myself in campaigning.

Recent headlines, however, have inspired me to become politically involved in the democratic process. In 2016, I participated in organized phone calls and mailings to support candidates in whom I believed. Two years later, I continue to be an activist. I participate in a grassroots organization to effect change at a local level. I contact my legislators on a regular basis through phone calls, emails, and letters. In addition, I have met with my United States representative, worked on post card campaigns, written postcards to encourage voter participation in recent off-year special elections, and provided financial support to organizations and publications that support my views. Even though these efforts are often met with defeat and disappointment, at least I have made a sincere effort to make a difference.

In turn, I work to be more accepting of those whose political views differ from mine. I try to listen more carefully and non-judgmentally without rushing in with my own opinion. I have expanded my reading to include a wider range of media and publications in belief that my knowledge will help me better understand why people think like they do. Such research also gives me insight as to how the country and the world got to where it is today .Maybe—just maybe—if friends and family members talk and share and communicate, we can encourage our government to take a more bi-partisan approach.

Finally, I strive to be kind. Whether it be coaching a local Special Olympics track and field team with my husband; extending a smile to strangers, or offering a helping hand to those impacted by recent natural disasters, I believe individual acts of goodness can make a difference. "Not all of us can do great things," Mother Theresa said. "But we can do small things with great love."

The Shabbat prayer book in our synagogue includes the following meditation: "I harbor within—we all do—a vision of my highest self, a dream of what I could and should become. May I pursue this vision, labor to make real my dream."

Through my voice, my writings, and my actions, I hope to help repair the world—to make our country and this world a better place for our own and future generations. I welcome you to join me on this journey.

Adapted from "Living My Values
The Jewish World, April 5, 2017

Holding On Tight

Since the year that we met, my husband Larry and I attend Rosh Hashanah—the Jewish New Year—services. We hear the shofar, listen to melodies that we only hear on the High Holy Days, and greet our friends with L'Shana Tova—Have a good year!

Attending High Holy Day services as an adult is different from my experiences as a child growing up in Keeseville, a small upstate town of two thousand people about ninety minutes south of Montreal. My uncle Paul had opened Pearl's, one of a chain of small department stores he had established in Vermont and Upstate New York. He hired my father to manage it. Although my parents had both grown up in New York City in Jewish neighborhoods, they had lived most of their married life in overwhelmingly Christian communities. In 1952, however, they found themselves in a town where they were the *only* Jewish family except for a childless couple, a lawyer and his wife. The next Jewish family didn't move in until the mid-sixties.

To offset the effects of our non-Jewish environment, my parents immediately joined Congregation Beth Israel, a Reform temple in Plattsburgh. We attended High Holy Day services and, depending on the weather conditions for the fifteen-mile drive, Shabbat services on Friday night. Saturday services were only held for the boys' bar mitzvahs; all the girls were confirmed at age sixteen.

In addition to attending services, my parents were insistent on their children getting a Jewish education. For a span of twenty years, our father made the trip up Route 9 every Sunday with whatever number of his children between the ages of five to sixteen were taking religious school lessons. We would arrive in Plattsburgh a half hour early. Then Dad would take us to the newsstand across the street from the temple on Oak Street. He purchased the *New York Times* for himself and comic books for us, our perk for going to Sunday school. My brother Jay chose Superman; Laura and Bobbie, Archie and Richie Rich; and I, *Classics*

Illustrated. Dad would then wait for us in his idling car —it got cold in that parking lot in the winter—reading the paper and smoking Kents. Over the years, all of us learned Jewish history, customs, and ethics. Jay learned Hebrew for his bar mitzvah. The three of us girls' Hebrew education was limited to the six-word *Shema* and blessings over bread, candles and wine. When we got home from school, Mom would have an elaborate dinner waiting for us—brisket, roasted potatoes, candied carrots, pickles, and delicious spiced apples from a jar—another perk for our going to Sunday school.

As residents of Keeseville and members of a temple in Plattsburgh, we were caught between two worlds. As we did not live in Plattsburgh, we often viewed ourselves as outsiders at Temple Beth Israel. My mother, in particular, did not feel comfortable with many of the congregants. A daughter of poor Russian immigrants, she often felt inferior to those who were third or fourth generation German Jews who historically regarded themselves as more educated and refined than those from the *shtetls*—the small towns with large Jewish populations which existed in Central and Eastern Europe before the Holocaust.

The residents of Keeseville were generally welcoming to our family, and we rarely experienced anti-Semitism. There were moments, however, that are etched in my memory. My parents were usually included, but there were occasional "lost" invitations to events, and we knew some viewed us as different. On rare occasions, the insults were more direct. When I was around six years old, I was playing on my front lawn with my doll. A teenaged boy who lived up the street came by and, giving the Nazi goose salute, yelled "Heil Hitler!" I ran inside crying. Jay, four years older than I, ran out of the house to chase him down and punch him in the nose. When Jay was in high school, the local priest advised his young female parishioners that it was best not to date "Hebrews." Obviously, this did not help Jay's social life.

The High Holy Days emphasized this "otherness" even more strongly. We did not attend school on Rosh Hashanah and Yom Kippur. My father closed the store, an event worthy of coverage in the *Essex County Republican*. Jay, who played football for Keeseville Central, missed every game that fell on the two major fall holidays, again newsworthy enough to make the local paper.

Everyone in Keeseville knew that the Cohens celebrated their

Jewish High Holy Days, but I was still sensitive to our being the only children missing school. One Rosh Hashanah, I was pushing my doll carriage in front of the house when I was overcome with embarrassment. What if someone saw me and wondered if I were playing hooky? I went inside to avoid the potential scrutiny and a visit from the truancy officer.

My feeling of "otherness" continued as the seasons changed. Beginning in November, I often had to explain that Chanukah was not the "Jewish Christmas," and no, we didn't have a Christmas tree or a Chanukah bush. As soon as we returned to school from the Thanksgiving break, the music classes I attended and, later, the choruses I joined in junior senior high were filled with Christmas music. I could handle "Little Town of Bethlehem" and "Deck the Halls." When it came to the line in "Silent Night" which stated "Christ the Savior is born," however, I would just mouth the words. The token inclusion of the song "I Had a Little Dreidel" didn't make me feel that the school was sensitive to my religion and culture

Other events brought their challenges. Passover often fell around Easter, and I watched my Christian friends devour bunny shaped chocolate eggs and jelly beans while I nibbled on my dry matzoh and butter. Once again, I felt different. In high school, my World History textbook reduced the Holocaust to the iconic 1943 picture from the Warsaw Ghetto of a German soldier pointing his machine gun at a little boy, clad in a coat with the yellow star, holding up his hands in terror. I can still remember looking down and crying silent tears while the teacher quietly and sympathetically moved on to the next topic. I understood clearly that the horror of the persecution of the Jews was diminished by this negligible treatment of the Holocaust in our textbook.

For many years, I saw other Jewish children mostly at Sunday School. As I got older, I joined a Jewish youth group and finally had Jewish friends. For the most part, however, our friends were our Christian classmates from Keeseville. We all dated in high school, but my parents pressed upon us their wish we would leave Keeseville after we graduated and make our lives in settings with more Jewish people.

In part because of my desire to be with other Jews, I enrolled in University of Albany in 1968. While at college, I attended High Holy Day services at Congregation Beth Emeth, but that was the extent of my Jewish participation until I met my future husband in 1973.

Larry and I attended High Holy Day services at Congregation Shaara TFille, the then-Orthodox *shul*—synagogue—in Saratoga to which his family belonged. What a dramatic difference for me! Men sat in the center pews, and the women, although not behind a *mehitzah,* (a curtain which separated the men from the women), sat in the back or on the sides. Most of the service was in Hebrew, and everyone prayed at what seemed to be lightning speed. Page numbers that were displayed on a chart on the bima provided my only means of following along with the prayer book. The services were much longer than those at Temple Beth Israel, and even the rabbis, with their black beards, *payots* (side curls), and *yarmulkes* (skull caps), were strange to me. In many ways, it was as foreign to me as the churches I had attended on occasion with my Christian friends.

After Larry and I were married, we bought a home in Clifton Park, a suburb of Albany, New York, in part because we knew that a synagogue had recently been built in the community. We joined in 1983, and we found that the Conservative service was a good compromise between Larry's Orthodox shul and my Reform temple. Ten years later, I celebrated my own bat mitzvah on my father's eightieth birthday, my way of honoring his commitment to our Jewish education.

Throughout my life, people assume that I, like many Jews, was brought up "downstate," in New York City or Long Island. When I tell them about growing up in Keeseville, they comment, "That must have been hard!"

It had its challenges, but it also offered wonderful opportunities. I grew up in a loving, close knit family, developed lifelong friendships, and enjoyed the beauty of Lake Champlain and the Adirondacks. I proudly identify myself as an Upstate New Yorker, with roots still entwined in that tiny town an hour south of the Canadian border.

Because of my unique upbringing, rather than losing my Jewish identity, my faith grew stronger. I could never take being a Jew for granted. And having a faith I had to hold on so tightly to maintain makes each High Holy Day, each Jewish milestone, even sweeter.

The Jewish World, August 29, 2013

New Year, Old Traditions

In September 2014, Larry and I hosted our annual Rosh Hashanah dinner in our home in Upstate New York. I made my traditional dishes: chicken in mushroom and wine sauce, brisket, roasted potatoes, honeyed carrots, challah, and mandel bread. My guests—all twenty-five of them—brought their favorites: chopped liver, cole slaw, broccoli casserole, fresh fruit, rugelach, a box of Kraus' chocolate, and a huge box of Jelly Belly jelly beans.

We had hosted Rosh Hashanah dinner every year since Larry's mother Doris passed away in 1994. It had become a tradition, dinner at my house immediately following services on the first day of the Jewish New Year. To be honest, I looked forward to it with a mixture of pleasure and dread. I loved opening my home, but I always worried: Would I have enough food? Would the house be too small to accommodate the family and friends we invited? It always seemed to come together. By the next morning I was already tweaking the menu for 2015: a little less chicken, a little more brisket, no more cookies.

Neither my husband and I nor my guests realized that the dinner would be the last one we hosted in our home in Upstate New York. Less than a year later, we were in a new home in Florida with new friends in a new synagogue.

Time for new traditions! Three months after we moved to Florida we hosted a Rosh Hashanah dinner for two couples at our large dining room table. The next year, several couples shared in the holiday preparations and pulled together a huge dinner with our own specialties.

In 2017, one of the women proposed a radical change. "We are in Florida! We are retired! Let's have our dinner catered!" Thanks to Too Jays, a local restaurant, we had a feast delivered to our door. Soup! Chopped liver! Brisket! Chicken! Tzimmes! Black and white cookies! We were amazed and delighted to find that everything was delicious, and no one had to cook or bake. Another new tradition!

One tradition I *will* maintain is that this time of year will be a personal period of self-reflection. We Jews are fortunate as we get to celebrate New Year's twice. The secular New Year, celebrated on January 1, is a time for late night parties and resolutions. My secular resolutions are qualitative: I will write one hour a day. I will walk thirty-five miles a week. I will lose twenty pounds. I will read one hundred books. My goals are concrete and precise and, especially the one regarding weight loss, recycled and retried and usually not achieved.

In the weeks prior to the High Holy Days and during my time in synagogue, my intentions have nothing to do with numbers and quantity. Instead, I focus on how I can improve the quality of my life, how I can become a better person than I was during the previous year before.

A prayer quoted by my rabbi in Upstate New York during a High Holy Day service read: "May I always find joy in scaling new mountains. May I never rest from my pursuit of knowledge. May I always desire to be a little better yesterday and a little bit less than tomorrow." With the abundance of problems that currently beset our country and our world, it is more important than ever for me to become more than I had been the previous year.

One way for me to move in that direction is to grow spiritually. Each year I vow not only to attend services but also to listen and reflect on the prayers and the rabbi's comments. I also aim to learn more about Judaism, about Israel, and our place in the world. I hope to share Sabbath dinners with old and new friends, lighting the candle sticks my grandfather carried from Russia and maybe even eating challah I made myself from my friend Flo's recipe. Practicing and appreciating the rituals of my faith tie me to my roots, my heritage.

And most importantly, I think about what I can do this coming year to leave the world a better place. The opportunities are endless. Extend a smile to strangers. Offer a helping hand to those impacted by recent natural disasters. Make contributions to organizations that support my values. Continue to subscribe to publications that share my views. Volunteer my time to causes in which I support. I believe these individual acts of goodness can make a difference.

In the *Mahzor Hadash* prayer book we use at Congregation Beth Shalom, one of my favorite prayer reads, "You have given us the ability to become more than we have been, the urge to be more than we are, and a gnawing hunger to attain heights only dimly imagined. For the power to grow, we give thanks." That to me is the essence of Rosh Hashanah. *L'Shanah Tova!* Happy New Year!

The Jewish World, September 3, 2015

I Can See Clearly Now

"**B**lessed are You, Adonai our G_d, Ruler of the universe, who opens the eyes of the blind." *Jewish Morning Blessing*

As our congregation recited the prayer on Rosh Hashanah in September 2017, this line in the traditional morning prayers took on deeper meaning. After struggling with extremely poor vision since elementary school, I no longer had to rely on corrective lenses. As Johnny Nash sang, "I can see clearly now."

No one was surprised when I was fitted for my first pair of glasses when I was six years old. Nearsightedness was prevalent in my family, and my parents and two older siblings were already wearing glasses. My vision, however, was complicated by amblyopia, a condition when the vision in one of the eyes is reduced because the eye and the brain are not working together properly. In my case, the right eye wandered toward the extreme right. In 1956, surgery was not an option. Instead, I was given a black patch to wear on my left eye to force the "lazy eye" to get stronger.

I wish my parents had been more persistent, but I was embarrassed and defiant. I refused to wear the patch. The vision in my right eye continued to deteriorate, and my left eye also was severely nearsighted. By the time I was in junior high school, my glasses were noticeably thick, only adding to the self-consciousness of teenager who also suffered from acne and what I perceived as a Jewish nose. When I was sixteen, an ophthalmologist told me my myopia was too severe for contact lens and predicted I would be blind by my twenties. He then fit me with a pair of glasses with lenses so thick, I looked as if I were looking through the bottoms of two soda bottles. When I got home, I threw them across the room and cried myself to sleep.

By the time I was a senior in high school, I was fitted for another pair of glasses by another less pessimistic eye doctor with lighter material that were not as ugly. But in my yearbook picture, the lenses all but hid my eyes.

When I arrived at the University at Albany, I was understandably self-conscious of my thick glasses. One time, my roommates thought it would be funny to hide my glasses when I was in the shower. I burst into tears and begged them to help me find them, as I didn't have sufficient sight to search for them.

My embarrassment regarding my vision hit its lowest moment when my girlfriend's cute but clueless boyfriend didn't respond to me when I was talking to him.

"Gene," Linda said, "Marilyn asked you a question."

"How was I supposed to know?" he answered. "Her glasses are so thick I can't even tell if she is looking at me."

At the end of my freshman year, I was experiencing frequent headaches. Doctors at the University at Albany health center referred me to a local ophthalmologist. "You are extremely near-sighted," the doctor stated. "Have you ever considered contact lenses?" I wasn't going blind! I was a candidate for contacts! I was measured, fitted, and scheduled to pick them up the second week of summer break.

I will never forget the day I first put those tiny hard lenses in my eyes. I walked outside and saw the leaves on the trees in all their beauty. The world was crystal clear. For the first time in my life, my eyes were causing tears of joy.

The lenses not only improved my vision but also my self-confidence. Behind those Coke bottles were my family's 'Pearlman' eyes, eyes the deepest color of blue. Helped a little by the blue tint on my lenses, my eyes became my best feature. "Has anyone ever told you that you have the most beautiful blue eyes?" strangers would tell me. "Yes, they have!" I would reply. "But you can tell me again!"

For the next fifty years, contact lenses were an integral part of my life. I popped them in the minute I woke up in the morning, and I popped them out just before I went to sleep. I was literally blind without them, but the world was a bright, sharp 20/20 with them.

Regular eye appointments kept me on track, and I used my glasses only when absolutely necessary. LASIK eye surgery was not an option for many years because of the severity of my myopia. When the surgery was perfected, my doctor suggested I wait. My family history, which had predicted corrective lenses, also predicted a high chance of the development of cataracts, a common eye problem seen in over fifty percent of the population by the age of eighty.

When I moved to Florida, I immediately established myself with a local eye doctor. In 2015, he told me that I had the beginning of cataracts. By the following spring, the cataract in my right eye, which had been deemed as "insignificant" only months before, was growing fast and was negatively impacting my vision. As soon as my husband Larry and I returned from our summer travels, I scheduled the surgery for the last week of September.

By Rosh Hashanah services less than a week after the procedure, I was able to greet fellow congregants, see the rabbi on the *bima*, the platform in front of the synagogue, and follow the entire service in our prayer books with no corrective lens in my right eye and my faithful contact lens in my left. The follow-up appointment confirmed that my right eye was a nearly perfect 20/25. After surgery for the cataract in my left eye was completed two months later, I was free of the corrective lenses I had needed for over sixty years.

Because of my poor vision, I have never felt confident climbing up the steps to the huge slides at water parks. As soon as I had medical clearance, however, I went down a huge slide on the Carnival cruise ship Larry and I sailed on after surgery. Who knows what's next? Sky diving? Why not? I can see clearly now. Wheeeee!

The Jewish World, October 11, 2016

Who By Fire, Who By Water?

During Yom Kippur, the Jewish Day of Atonement, we recite the *Unetaneh Tokef,* a prayer in which we ask G_d to inscribe us in the Book of Life for the coming year. The prayer took on special significance for my husband Larry and me in 2016 as we looked back on our experiences with our first Florida hurricane.

The National Hurricane Center had been tracking Hurricane Irma since late August. Reports of its potential destructive path through the Caribbean and Florida were headline news by Labor Day. Despite the warnings, Larry and I decided to go ahead with our planned trip to visit an aunt in Myrtle Beach. On Tuesday, September 5, we drove to St. Augustine, Florida, for a day of touring before driving the rest of the way to South Carolina. We were confident that we had plenty of time to return home by Friday to prepare for Irma's predicted landfall that weekend.

That confidence quickly faded. News of the devastation in the Caribbean from Irma was being updated hourly. On the streets of St. Augustine, fellow tourists and residents, some who had just recently moved back into homes that had been damaged by Hurricane Matthew in 2016, were on their cell phones making evacuation plans. We filled our car with gas moments before the pumps ran dry. We stopped at the supermarket for some basics, only to find that the bread and water aisles were picked clean. Continuing north was out of the question. We drove back your home south of Orlando the next morning.

By that time, Larry and I were being bombarded with phone calls, texts, emails, and Facebook posts from worried family and friends. Were we okay? Were we going to evacuate? We assured them that we were fine and were staying put. Our homes were built to withstand hurricane winds and rain, and Central Florida was not subject to storm surges. Furthermore, we were not targeted to be in the path of the storm. We were more concerned about our family and friends who lived and/or owned homes on the coasts of Florida. Which coast? As of Saturday, meteorologists were *still* trying to determine where the monster storm would make landfall.

So we, like millions of other Floridians, completed all the necessary preparations. We stocked up on water, canned goods, toilet paper and wine—lots of wine. We filled both cars with gas. We brought everything from our lanai and in our yard into our house and garage. We pulled out our emergency crank radio, candles and matches, flashlights and batteries. We filled our bathtubs and large pots with water and our freezer with bags of ice. We prepared a "safe room" in a walk-in closet in case of extreme winds or tornadoes. We checked in with neighbors to see if they needed help getting ready. And we watched the "spaghetti models" on The Weather Channel for hours. *Stupefacente*! (Amazing in Italian)

Speaking of amazing, in between all these preparations, Larry and I were still living our lives—the calm before the storm. We went to the movies, celebrated our anniversary with dinner and champagne, took long walks around the neighborhood, and even went to a Pre-Hurricane Irma party on Saturday night.

On Sunday morning, we hunkered down and waited for Irma's expected landfall on—we were told—Florida's west coast. Winds began to pick up outside our windows in the afternoon, followed by several hours of torrential rains and strong gusts. Around midnight, just when we thought the worst was over, The Weather Channel announced that Irma was changing course. She was veering farther east and going over Polk County—sixty miles from our house. The next two hours were terrifying—at least for me. Larry had gone to sleep before the warning was issued. By two a.m., with wind gusts reaching between 74 and 100 miles per hour, I woke Larry and begged him to join me in our safe room. Larry refused, so I spent the next hour huddled in the closet with my laptop while Larry snored ten feet away. Once the winds calmed down, I joined Larry in our now safe bed.

By late the next morning, the weather had improved enough for us to venture outside. Our house was intact. Outside of a few missing shingles and some small downed trees, it appeared that our entire community had made it through the hurricane without serious damage. We never lost power or water. We had survived Irma! We even saved a catfish that was flopping in the gutter at the end of our driveway by tossing it back into the lake.

Our relief was short-lived. We quickly learned of the extent of destruction outside our community. Millions of people across Florida were without power and water. Homes and businesses were damaged or destroyed. In Polk County alone, eighty percent of homes were without electricity.

In the weeks that followed Irma, Larry and I questioned how such different scenarios could exist only a few hours or even blocks apart. Disney World and Universal opened for business as usual the day after the storm while people who lived on the Florida Keys could not even get back to their homes to assess the damage for at least a week. Residents of our community were playing mah jongg, watching movies, and doing yoga while friends in Naples and Boca Raton were dealing with gas shortages, mold, extreme heat, and sewage back-up. A member of our neighborhood blog wrote a post complaining about his recyclables not being picked up when, less than a mile away, residents near our 55+ community were waiting in long lines for water and FEMA packages.

Fortunately, most members of our community, joining like-minded residents throughout Central Florida, pitched in to help. Many opened up their homes to friends and family until the victims could return to their homes. Several clubs collected food, water, and money to aid people who worked in our community but lived in the affected areas. Many contributed to organizations such as the American Red Cross, Habitat for Humanity, and the Jewish Federation of Florida.

Who by water and who by fire? We were spared from serious consequences, but others weren't. Now it is our responsibility as Jews, as human beings, to help others through *tzedakah*—through charity—to relieve the burden of the thousands of others who were not so fortunate

The Jewish World, September 28, 2017

The Candle Debacle

Growing up as the only Jewish family in our small upstate town of Keeseville had its challenges. Most people were accepting, but at times we Cohens felt like outsiders. Unfortunately for me, one of the worst experiences I ever experienced resulted from problems that arose when I *was* included.

As many of the Catholic children attended a parochial school through sixth grade, most of my friends in the public school were Methodists. We were a close group, sharing not only the classroom but also dinners and sleep-overs at each other's homes. Knowing I was Jewish was never an issue, and my friends were happy to share my holidays and to invite us to share theirs.

While my classmates in Keeseville were Christian, I also had a group of Jewish classmates at the synagogue in Plattsburgh to which my family belonged. I rarely saw them outside of synagogue as the shul was fifteen miles north of us. As they and their families lived near each other and socialized with each other, I considered them acquaintances but certainly not close friends. As a matter of fact, I fancied myself as the Country Mouse in our little town compared to their City Mouse existence in the big metropolis of Plattsburgh. I lived in two different worlds: my Jewish life consisting of Sunday school and Friday night services in Plattsburgh, and my secular life consisting of public school and close friendships in Keeseville.

When we were in sixth grade, the local Methodist church had a special event planned for their youth. Two sisters, elderly and either widowed or never married, offered their home to have a weekly get-together in which each of the participants was to make Christmas candles. The mothers of the girls called my mother and asked if I could join them. My mother gave her permission. Glad to be included, I joined the group despite some discomfort that I, the Jewish girl, was participating in a Christmas activity.

Once a week for four weeks, the eight of us climbed the stairs to the ladies' apartment above one of the stores on Front Street. We melted wax and crayons and then dipped strings into the hot liquid. The two ladies then hung up the candles, let them dry, and had them ready for us the following week. While my Christian friends created layers of red and green wax and decorated their creations with holly, I chose blue and white hues for my candles in honor of Chanukah.

On the last day of our candle making adventure, we met at the usual time and began putting on the final touches of our masterpieces. One of the ladies announced that she had a special surprise. The church had contacted the *Plattsburgh Press Republican* and asked them to do a holiday story about our candle making project. "The newspaper's reporter will be coming this afternoon to take pictures and interview you all for the article," she said. "Isn't that exciting?"

It may have been exciting for my friends, but I immediately panicked. What if my Jewish friends saw me in a photograph with a group of Methodists making Christmas candles? Would they look at me unfavorably, as a further outsider to their life in Plattsburgh? I decided I could not be in the picture. I feared it would be a public statement that I joined Christians in their religious school/church events—a *shanda*—a shame on me and my family

"Thank you very much," I said to the two ladies. "But I don't want to be in the picture."

"What do you mean?" one of the ladies asked.

"I don't want to be in the picture," I replied. "I enjoyed making the candles, but I don't want my name in the newspaper. If my Jewish friends in Plattsburgh see it, they will think I'm not acting like a Jew."

I grabbed my candle and left. Little did I know what havoc I had wrought.

By that evening, my mother had received several phone calls from my friends' mothers. My "rude" actions indicated to them that I ashamed of associating with Christians. As a result, I had not only embarrassed not only myself but also my parents and siblings, the only Jewish family in our town.

My mother, who was angry and upset, told me that she agreed with the other mothers. My father, however, understood. "You learned a lesson from this, Marilyn," he told me. "Never put yourself in any situation in which you feel uncomfortable and would feel ashamed."

Fortunately for all of us Cohens, the tempest I created calmed down fairly soon. My friends certainly forgot about it, and the adults moved on to more current kerfuffles in our small town. Peace and goodwill returned.

Decades later, I still look back on this incident with remorse, especially for bringing the wrath of the Keeseville Methodists down on my mother's head. I now have a more mature perspective: I appreciate how difficult it was for me as a child of to reconcile the need to be accepted by my Christian friends while not betraying my Jewish heritage.

I haven't had anymore "candle debacles" since that incident in Keeseville. This doesn't mean that I still don't struggle with the holiday season. I, along with many of my fellow Jews, still walk a fine line between sharing the joy of the holidays while maintaining my Jewish identity. It's a dilemma I initially faced as a child and continue to face today.

The Jewish World, November 26, 2015

Finding the Perfect Gift

I have never looked forward to holiday shopping.
It has little to do with spending the money. I don't even resent the time in the malls with all the Christmas decorations and music and the token Chanukah menorah stuck sadly in a corner. My main problem is that I never feel up to the task of finding the "perfect" gift.

I have a few memories of shopping for the holidays when I was growing up. I had my standbys: Evening in Paris perfume for my mother, a carton of cigarettes and a bar of chocolates for my father. When my sister Laura came home from college at winter break during her freshman year, she gave me a thick, beige cable sweater. I viewed the gift as the height of sophistication because it came from my "big sister." Through my college years, finding funny and appropriate gifts for my suite mates made the days before we left for winter vacation enjoyable.

It became more challenging once I married into Larry's family. Chanukah was a much bigger deal than it had been in my family. My siblings and I had not exchanged Chanukah gifts for years. Now I was looking for presents for ten adults and the seven grandchildren. Even if we weren't all together on the first night of Chanukah, Larry's sisters seemed to know what to get everyone and have it delivered by mail if necessary. I wondered what to get everyone and second-guessed all my choices.

Gift giving became even more complicated in 2000 when I moved from the classroom into an administrative post at our adult education facility. When I was teaching, I participated in a Secret Santa exchange, which meant I was only finding little gifts for one person. Once I took on administrative position, the number of people to whom I gave gifts grew exponentially. It would have been simpler if I had been a wonderful baker or a clever seamstress or a skilled woodcrafter. Unfortunately, I had neither the talent nor the desire to pull together a "one gift fits all" idea and implement it by the time the holiday season arrived. Gifts reflecting my own holiday—sugar cookies in the shapes of menorahs and Star of Davids; potato pancakes ready to reheat; a Chanukah bag with a *dreidel,* the symbolic tiny top inscribed with Hebrew letter, Chanukah *gelt* (chocolate coins), and instructions on how to play the traditional game—seemed inappropriate.

I would wander around malls or craft shows the weeks before the holiday searching desperately for gifts. I truly cared about the recipients and wanted to show that caring in what I chose for each person. I just was at a lost to find a small present for everyone that satisfied me.

Four years before I retired, I decided keep track of the financial impact on buying holiday presents for my co-workers. I was shocked to realize that I had spent $500 on *tchotchkes*—little nothings. This had to stop.

So the following November, before Thanksgiving and the beginning of the holiday shopping season, I approached my fellow administrators. I asked if we could forego the gifts and instead make a contribution to a charity. They quickly signed on. For the next few years, we pooled our gift money and sent a generous check to the Regional Food Bank. Everyone at my agency got a card with a note that said, in the spirit of the season, a gift had been made to feed the hungry. What a relief!

The December after I retired, the holiday season was comparatively mellow. Larry's family got together for a Chanukah dinner, with all of us agreeing beforehand that Chanukah presents would be purchased for the two great-grandchildren but not for the adults. We have continued that tradition.

My perspective on gift-giving also changed in 2015. Larry and I purchased a fully furnished home in Florida, and we needed to divest ourselves of thirty-six years of house. Larry took it in stride. I struggled with the process until I realized much "stuff" we decided to leave behind was someone else's treasure. The couple that cleaned our house fell in love with a chalk drawing of a draw bridge in Shushan, New York. She and her husband had driven over it every day when they lived in Columbia County and were thrilled when we gifted it to them. Several of my crewel pieces found their way to relatives' homes, and a photograph of waves crashing on a New England coastline went to a dear friend whose family has had a summer home near Brunswick,

Maine, since 1925. Our Early American deacon's bench was moved into our next door neighbors' sunroom. Moments before we backed out of our driveway on Devon Court for the last time, Blossom took a picture of the two of us on the bench, smiling through our tears. How I wish I had gifts from the heart to offer to friends and family all the time no matter what the season!

Now that we have a grandchild, my initial inclination is to shop for eight gifts to be opened each night. I know at her young age, Sylvie Rose doesn't need more toys or more clothes. I have already promised her that, when she is older, I will take her to Disney World and buy her a princess dress. Meanwhile, I have children's books written and signed by a member of my writing group to give to her. My journal includes stories of her life, and I hope to share all these stories, some as part of my books, with her as she grows. Those will be, like those special pictures and that deacon's bench—gifts from the heart.

The Jewish World, November 12, 2015

"May the Force Be With You!"

During the eight days of Chanukah, in between candle lighting and potato latkes, my husband Larry and I will celebrate a Shapiro tradition: We will go to see the newest *Star Wars* film. We have been fans since Adam caught the *Star Wars* bug as a toddler from a future stormtrooper.

In September 1979, I began substitute teaching two to three days a week at our local high school. We left Adam in the care of a wonderful baby sitter, Sandy Harris, who lived just down the street.

Adam was seventeen months old and just beginning to talk. His vocabulary consisted of a few words—*mamma, dadda,* and *apple dus* (juice).

Less than a month later, however, Adam shocked us by announcing at the dinner table, "I know Star Wars."

"You know Star Wars?" Larry asked, astonished.

"Yes," said Adam. "Luke Skywalker. Han Solo. Princess Leia. Chewbacca."

And Adam continued to prattle on, clearly stating the names of numerous characters from the *Star Wars* movies.

It didn't take us long to figure out where Adam had picked up his expanded vocabulary. Sandy's twelve-year-old son Timmy had been enthralled with George Lucas' blockbuster since the first film in the franchise was released in 1977. Kenner Toys had the license to make the related toys, and Timmy had collected them all. He set the little action figures and their spaceships on shelves in his room, recreating scenes from the original movie and its sequel, *The Empire Strikes Back*. When he came home from school, Timmy would entertain his mother's charge by allowing him to play with his collection. Adam was hooked.

That Chanukah, Larry and I purchased several action figures and a replica of the space ship Millennium Falcon for Adam. He got more for his second birthday and the following Chanukah. Although he had yet to see the movie, his interest and ability to recreate scenes using his collection and available toys as props—blocks, Legos, even a blanket on top of a milk crate—amazed us.

In April 1981, Larry and I planned a surprise for Adam for his third birthday. While I stayed home with his one-month-old sister, Larry took Adam to see a re-release of the original *Star Wars* film. Adam had never been to a movie theater, and he had no idea why he and his father were sharing a box of popcorn in a huge room filled with people sitting in chairs facing a screen. The minute the music started and the opening credits rolled, however, Adam knew exactly what was happening. Our three-year-old was transfixed for the entire length of the film.

Over the next few years, Adam watched and re-watched the first two movies and, in 1983, *The Return of the Jedi*. As the franchise expanded, Adam's *Star Wars* collection expanded—sometimes with his help.

When he was around four years old, Adam asked us if he could get a new Luke Skywalker as the light saber was missing. We refused, saying he could use a toothpick or a prop from another character. A few days later, Adam brought us a headless Luke.

"It fell off," he explained. "Can I get a new one?"

So we replaced Luke, only to have Adam bring us a few days later a headless stormtrooper, one of the white armored minions of the evil Empire. When the head of bounty hunter Boba Fett also went missing, we realized that Adam was biting the heads off to get us to purchase a complete toy. His gig was up.

Adam's passion for *Star Wars* continued until he was nine years old, when his interest in science fiction expanded to *Star Trek* and Tolkien's *Lord of the Rings* Trilogy. The action figures and a couple of space ships were relegated to a box in the closet. By the time the series was revived in 1999, Adam was in college. On his visits home, he would occasionally open up the box, reminisce, and put them back on the shelf.

In January 2015, Larry and I came back from a trip to Florida to sub-zero temperatures, twelve inches of snow on the front yard, and a broken mailbox, the victim of the town snowplow. A day after a call into town hall, I noticed that a Clifton Park service truck was parked at the end of the driveway. I opened the door to be greeted by no other than Timmy Harris, whom I had not seen in at least twenty years.

"I'm here to fix your mailbox, Mrs. Shapiro," Timmy said after our initial greetings. "But before I do that, I have to ask you a question. My mother has told me for years that because of me, Adam's first words were the names of *Star Wars* action figures. Is that true?"

I assured him it was and recounted the story of that night over thirty-five years ago when Adam's vocabulary increased exponentially.

"Are you still a *Star Wars* fan?" I asked Timmy.

"Absolutely!" Timmy responded. "I have a two bedroom house, with one room devoted to forty years of *Star Wars* collectibles. My favorite pieces are still the Kenner toys from the late 70's."

Not only is Timmy still a fan, but also he is part of the 501st Legion, "Vader's Fist," an international costuming group that "troops" as the bad guy characters from Star Wars. Along with his fellow members, Timmy dresses up as both as a stormtrooper and as Boba Fett.

The 501st's main function is as a charity organization. In 2015 alone $587,000 was donated on its behalf to various children's charities including Make-A-Wish Foundation, Ronald McDonald houses, and local pediatric hospitals. The "bad guys doing good" are also found at science fiction and comic book conventions and every *Star Wars* film openings.

"*Star Wars* costuming is gratifying on a few levels." Timmy later shared with me, "I get to contribute to something worthwhile. And as a 49-year-old man who dresses up as a plastic spaceman, I get to be a nine-year-old again. That's worth all of the time, sweat and armor pinches that we go though."

When Larry and I moved to Florida in June 2015, Adam requested we send him only a few items from the house—two Adirondack photographs and a Monet print, his yearbooks, and the *Star Wars* action figures. And like his parents, he too will be watching the newest *Star Wars* over his holiday break.

Happy Chanukah, and may the force be with you!

The Jewish World, December 8, 2016

Friends, Fried Rice, and Fortune Cookies

On December 23, 2017, Larry and I traveled 400 miles to spend time with our friends Chris and Bernie Grossman in their new home in Tallahassee, Florida. On December 25, the Shapiros and Grossmans upheld a tradition as steeped in Jewish culinary ritual as eating brisket on Rosh Hashanah, potato latkes (pancakes) on Chanukah, and matzo ball soup on Passover. We would be eating Chinese food on Christmas Day.

Growing up in a small town in Upstate New York, my family didn't eat Chinese food out on Christmas Day, or any day of the year. If there was a Chinese restaurant in Plattsburg, the "big town" near us, I don't remember ever going there. Most of the time, LaChoy canned dinners from Grand Union were the closest we got to Asian cuisine.

Once or twice a year, however, my father would pile my mother and the four children into the station wagon and drive the ninety miles to Montreal. We would weave our way into Chinatown and head to the Nanking Cafe. We would climb a set of steep stairs and crowd around a table in a booth. The wonton soup and noodles would be followed by chicken chow mein or moo shu shrimp—much better than the stuff we ate out of cans. (Family lore tells of the time that my brother Jay drank the water in the finger bowl.) We would finish up with fortune cookies and vanilla ice cream and head back home. To be honest, that was the extent of our seeing Montreal until I visited the World's Fair in 1968.

The Chinese food at Christmas tradition started for me after Larry and I married and bought a home in Saratoga County in 1976. Ling's, near the corner of Routes 146 and 9 in Clifton Park, was the only restaurant open on December 25. (It was also the only Chinese restaurant in a ten mile radius; there are now at least ten!) Larry and I met half the Jewish population of our community there.

By the next year, we were going to Ling's with a group of friends. And by the time our children left home, we had a standing date for a

December 25 dinner with the Grossmans and several other couples in various Chinese restaurants throughout the Capital District. Wherever we chose to go, we could count on sharing the evening with tables of fellow Jews—including many rabbis and their families.

The tradition continued when we moved to Florida in 2015. The Grossmans and another of our regulars, Joyce and Mel Toub, joined us in Kissimmee for three days in late December. Of course, we had reservations at the local Chinese restaurant on Christmas Day.

In 2016, Chanukah started on December 24. Congregation Shalom Aleichem in Kissimmee held a community dinner. I was hoping we would be dining on huge metal pans filled with vegetarian or kosher style dishes from one of the two Chinese restaurants close to our shul. To my disappointment, the committee planning the event opted for Italian. The next day, we joined my brother Jay, his wife Leslie, and their family for a traditional Chanukah meal in Sarasota. In 2017, however, we were back on track for wonton and moo shu, heading to Tallahassee to maintain the ritual of eating Chinese food on December 25.

According to Mathew Goodman, author of *Jewish Food: The World at Table*, the Jews' love for Chinese food dates back over one hundred years ago. The Lower East Side of Manhattan was populated by Eastern European Jews, Italian, and Chinese. "Italian cuisine and especially Italian restaurants, with their Christian iconography, held little appeal for Jews," Mark Tracy wrote in a 2011 Atlantic article. "But the Chinese restaurants had no Virgin Marys. And they prepared their food in the Cantonese culinary style, which utilized a sweet-and-sour flavor profile, overcooked vegetables, and heaps of garlic and onion"—all similar to Eastern European cuisine.

Another theory was included in a 1992 academic (seriously!) paper by Gayle Tuchman and Harry G. Levine in which they supported the idea that Chinese food was 'Safe Treyf.' True the dishes featured unkosher foods including shellfish and pork. But it was chopped and minced and mixed with so many vegetables, it was disguised. As stated in a 2007 blog post *Feed the Spirit*, "If pork was in wontons (which looked very much like Jewish kreplach) or in tiny pieces in chop suey, it didn't seem as bad as chowing down on a ham sandwich. And the Chinese typically don't cook with dairy products, so no one had to worry about mixing milk and meat."

The concept has made it to the highest court in our country. According to the *Judaism 101* website, Justice Elena Kagan brought up the Jewish/Chinese food connection up at her 2010 Supreme Court confirmation hearing. When a senator asked her where she was on Christmas, she said, "You know, like all Jews, I was probably at a Chinese restaurant."

In 2009, Brandon Miller even penned a song: "I eat Chinese food on Christmas/Go to the movie theater, too/'Cause there just ain't much else to do on Christmas/When you're a Jew."

As you can tell by her undecidedly non-Jewish name, Chris was not born Jewish. She converted after she met Bernie at Grinnell College in Iowa, and keeps kosher in and out of the home. So on December 25, in a Chinese restaurant in Tallahassee, she ordered the egg drop soup and General Tso's tofu.

The rest of us, however, ate "Safe Treyf." Larry ordered shrimp with garlic sauce, Bernie got egg rolls and black pepper beef tenderloin tips ("Bernie always eats something with beef, no matter what ethnic variety food we have," quipped Chris). And I ordered my favorite—moo shu chicken with pancakes and plum sauce.

After the main meal, we popped open our fortune cookies and shared the Chinese predictions for the upcoming year. Then we went back to the Grossmans and dined on my "world famous chocolate chip cookies," another long-standing holiday tradition for us friends. We raised a glass of wine, shouted *L'Chaim (*To Life!) and *Ganbei* (gon bay) the traditional Chinese toast which literally means 'dry cup.'

In 2017, the Hebrew year was 5778 and the Chinese year was 4715. That must mean, the old joke goes, that against all odds the Jews went without Chinese food for 1,064 years. *Fortunate*-ly, for us, we again shared fried rice, friendship and fortune cookies with the Grossmans.

The Jewish World, December 28, 2017

The Holiday Card

The holidays are over. The greeting cards we find in our mailbox are slowing down to a dribble. Yet, I totally understand if they arrive even mid-January. I've had numerous years where good intentions to get all my cards signed, sealed and delivered before the first night of Chanukah or before Christmas Eve have failed.

We were fortunate to receive many lovely holiday cards from across the country throughout the holiday season. Most were simple but attractive ones from Hallmark or American Greetings. The two handmade cards, beautifully crafted pieces of art, were placed in my memory box, to be enjoyed again and again. Many greetings were in the form of photo cards: a picture of my great niece and nephew with their labradoodle; a three-generation photo from a childhood friend; a picture of two friends, Santa, and their "children"—two rescue dogs.

I especially appreciated cards that included a holiday newsletter that recapped the senders' year and shared what their family had been up in 2016. Reading about relatives, friends, and their loved ones, especially those that live far away from us, brought us closer together despite the miles between us.

Happily, this year, we did not receive any form of the 'Dreaded Holiday Letter.' You know the kind I mean. *Happy Holidays! We just bought a little present for ourselves. The red Ferrari is parked in the four-car garage next to the Lexus, the Maserati, and the Tesla. Of course we have to find the time to drive it as we will be working around our upcoming trip to the French Riviera and our two month cruise to South America on our yacht.*

Embarrassingly, I may have been guilty of putting a little too much enthusiasm in past holiday letters. The Shapiro Year in Review was contained in a single-spaced letter with a border of dreidels or menorahs. Before I mailed it out, I would ask Larry, my husband, and our children, Adam and Julie, to review it. Being more private people than me, they would eliminate much of what I considered news-worthy items. "Too much information!" they would comment. The edited letters were shorter and considerably less, well, Pollyannaish.

In 2015, I decided I wanted to go the photo card route. I created my masterpiece in a short time at the Walgreens kiosk with three pictures representing our year. One showed Larry and me posing with Phineas and Ferb at Disney World. Another was a picture of Julie and her husband Sam holding our one month old granddaughter Sylvie Rose in their backyard. The third was a picture of Adam holding Sylvie.

I didn't get them mailed by Chanukah, which started in early December, so I aimed for December 24. And then New Years. And then Martin Luther King's Birthday. By the end of January, I purchased cute little heart stickers to add to the photo with the intention of mailing them out by Valentine's Day. By April, I ruled out Easter egg stickers. The ten plague stickers I found on the internet seemed a little depressing.

Sylvie was now nine months old and looked nothing like the infant in the pictures. The photo cards went into the trash, and the odd-sized envelopes were used to mail bills that need to be paid.

Friends in England introduced us to the *Jacquie Lawson* website. For years, we have sent out its beautiful animated greeting cards for all occasions—birthdays, anniversaries, get well wishes, Valentine Day notes—to family members and friends.

I wasn't going to repeat the photo card disaster. In 2016, Larry and I decided to send the e-cards for the holidays. The Chanukah card, choreographed to *Chanukah Oh Chanukah,* transformed a lovely tree into a brightly lit menorah. Our non-Jewish friends received a card set to a medley of Christmas songs that tracked a sleigh making its way through a picture-perfect English village and surrounding countryside.

The first night of Chanukah fell on Christmas Eve, so it gave us extra time to get them ready to send out. Of course we procrastinated until December 24. Larry worked from his computer in the office sending out Christmas greetings to all who celebrated the Christian holiday while I worked from my laptop in the kitchen sending out Chanukah wishes to all who celebrated the Jewish holiday. By the time we left for the Chanukah party at our synagogue that evening, we had sent over one hundred cards with short personal notes to friends and family across the country and world.

I was a little concerned that the recipients would not bother to open them or, if they did, they would be bored with the forty seconds of animation. We were therefore happy to receive thank you notes back from most the recipients within hours—sometimes minutes—after we clicked the send button. The e-cards were a success!

Recently, I saw the following quote in a friend's kitchen: "Though time and miles may separate us, we have built a bridge of lovely memories to span the distance." No matter how we share our good wishes for the holidays, and no matter when those good wishes arrive, they all are sent and received with love and happiness.

The Jewish World, January 5, 2017

Disney Princesses and Purim Queens

According to an old Borscht Belt joke, all of Jewish holidays basically come down to one theme: "They tried to kill us. We survived. Let's eat!"

Purim follows the plot line: Haman, an evil advisor to King Ahasuerus, encourages him to kill all the Jews. The new queen Esther, with the help of her brother Mordecai, saves the day. We eat *hamantashen*—the traditional triangular pastry— and drink wine.

Purim has always been one of my favorite Jewish holidays. On March 18, 1973, Larry and I met at a Purim party organized by an Albany Jewish singles group. We were in a *shpiel*—skit—based on The Dating Game. He was King Ahasuerus; I was Queen Esther. Over hamantashen and punch, we discovered that we had a great deal in common and, unsaid, a mutual attraction. The rest is history.

But there is another reason I love the holiday: it is in many ways a fairy tale about kings and queens and love conquers all. When it comes to costume parties, most little girls want to be Esther. And I as a child was no exception. Each holiday, my mother would find a pretty robe, and I would make a crown out of cardboard and aluminum foil. *Voila!* I was royalty!

Much to my embarrassment, I still love a good romance where true love conquers all obstacles and the couple lives happily ever after. Some of my favorite movies—*Beauty and the Beast*, *You've Got Mail*, *Moonstruck*—carry that theme. When we moved to Florida, I emptied my book shelves, only taking enough to fill a small bookcase full of my favorites. Not surprising, many of them follow the same plot: *Jane Eyre*, *Pride and Prejudice*, and a dog-eared Golden book version of Walt Disney's *Cinderella*. I spent many an hour on my mother's lap listening to that story and its promise of happily ever after.

Now that we live only forty minutes from Disney World, I have had many opportunities to experience the "Princess Phenomenon." At stores throughout the parks, little girls can purchase Disney princess costumes. The Bibbidi Bobbidi Boutique offers salon services to "make one's little princess... look and feel like royalty." Throughout all the parks, Disney cast members—Disney's term for all their employees— sweep past us dressed up in as Cinderella, Snow White, and Sleeping Beauty. At scheduled times throughout the day, one can have a picture taken with favorite Disney characters. Mickey, Donald, and Pluto have their share of people waiting in line for their photo opportunity. The venues with the longest lines, however, are the ones for the princesses. I have not yet bought myself a "Cinderella" dress (I don't even think one can purchase them in adult sizes). But I gaze wistfully at the serpentine queues, hoping that someday I can persuade Larry to wait for me while I have my opportunity to share a photo with Belle or Ariel.

My fascination with princesses is small potatoes compared to many. According to wdw.com, over 1,200 couples a year tie the knot at Walt Disney World Resort. That is nothing to which to shake a magic wand! And I can't even begin to imagine the number of couples a year who honeymoon there. One can recognize them by the Disney Minnie Mouse bride and Mickey Mouse groom ear hat sets sported by many young couples.

What separates Queen Esther from many of the Disney princesses is that Esther is not just a passive maiden waiting for the magic kiss of her Price Charming. Rather, she is actively involved in saving the Jewish people. In the Purim story, King Ahashuarus banishes his first wife Vashti after she refuses to show off her beauty wearing just a crown to a banquet room full of men "merry with wine." After a search throughout the kingdom, Esther, a Jewish orphan, is chosen to be queen. The new bride learns from her Uncle Mordecai that Haman, the king's evil advisor, is plotting to kill all the Jews. Beguiling the king with her beauty at a banquet, Esther then reveals that she herself is a Jew and that her people are threatened.

On a 2015 visit to a Disney store, I saw an adorable princess outfit in a nine-month size, perfect for my infant granddaughter. I took a picture and sent it to my daughter. "What do you think?" I texted.

Julie called me back immediately. "Let's get one thing straight. My daughter is not going to be wearing any princess outfits."

To her relief, I told her that her father had already strongly encouraged me to put the princess outfit back on the store's display. I assured her for the immediate future I would limit my gift outfit choices to more acceptable themes, like hedgehogs or rainbows or, in honor of my son-in-law, the Denver Broncos.

However, I already have plans five years down the road of having Sylvie stay with me and whisking her off to Disney in a princess dress of her choosing. And the magical salon experience? Even I have reservations about the Bibbidi Bobbidi Boutique.

Or maybe, further in line with Julie's thinking, I will share with Sylvie the story of Purim. I will tell her about a woman who is plucked out of obscurity to become queen of a large kingdom. She gets the man and the crown. Rather than living "happily ever after," she uses her position to let good overcome evil. In the process, she became a Jewish heroine beloved centuries later. And that story doesn't require any magical kisses from Prince Charming.

The Jewish World March 17, 2016

Cutting It Close: The Passover Bris

Each year, as we prepare for Passover, my thoughts are not only on the upcoming holiday but also the memories of a special Passover almost forty years ago.

In early spring in 1978, Larry and I were anxiously awaiting for the birth of our first child. My mother and my older sister had delivered their babies early and easily, and I was expecting the same experience for me. It didn't turn out that way. After I had gone through several hours of unproductive labor, our baby was delivered on his due date, Saturday, April 15, by Caesarian section. Despite the unexpected surgery, Larry and I were absolutely thrilled. We had a perfect healthy little boy, our little tax deduction, our Adam Michael Shapiro.

Now that we had a son, we needed to plan a *bris*, the Jewish birth ceremony during which a baby boy is brought into the Covenant of the Jewish people. Unlike today's births, the average stay for a woman who delivered by C-section in the 1970s was eight days. We arranged to have the ceremony and celebration in one of the conference rooms in St. Peters Hospital on the following Sunday.

We then faced the difficulty of finding a rabbi and/or moyel. Sunday was the second full day of Passover. As a C-section was not considered a "natural birth," the holiday technically superseded the commandment of the ceremony on the eighth day. Fortunately, my brother and sister-in-law had a close friend who was the daughter of a local rabbi. He graciously agreed to officiate on *yontiff*, on the holiday. One of the doctors in my obstetrics/gynecology practice, who was Jewish, agreed to perform the duties of the *moyel*, the person who would complete the circumcision.

By the time we had set everything up, it was Friday, the first night of Passover. Larry was invited to a friend's home for the Seder, the symbolic Passover meal, and I had a decidedly un-Passover dinner in my hospital room. When one of the nurses came in to check on me, I commented that I thought I had developed a bed sore from lying around the hospital bed for the past six days. She took a look, and said, "That's not a bed sore. You've developed a pilonidal cyst on the bottom of your tailbone."

"What does that mean?" I asked.

"Well, I'm not a doctor," she started. "But you probably will have to have surgery to remove it. Then you will have to stay in the hospital for another week while it heals. Of course, as it is an infection, you will have to be in isolation and will be unable to take care of your baby until you are healed."

That did it for me. I was recovering from major surgery, we were planning on a bris on Sunday, and now I was facing additional hospital time. I did what any sane, sensible postpartum mother would do: I had a complete, hysterical melt-down. Unfortunately and to add to the drama, Larry was at a Seder at a friend's place who had an unlisted number. It took some effort to get the phone operator to agree to contact Larry and then have him call me back. Once he was reached, Larry left his friend's house mid-seder and drove back to the hospital to comfort me. The next morning, my doctor assured me that a good dose of antibiotics would work in the short run, with surgery only an option down the road if necessary. The bris was still on, and it was time for us to focus on the celebration.

The day of the bris, my mother and mother-in-law came with Passover wines, cakes and cookies, along with fresh fruit. They covered the tables with white table cloths and used an extra one to cover the crucifix that was hanging on the wall of the Catholic-affiliated hospital. Our family was all there, the rabbi was sweet and kind, and the doctor who performed the circumcision was steady handed. The adults, including the father and mother, handled the procedure calmly. The most attentive guest was our five-year-old niece Katie, who took an unusually close-up interest in the procedure. When asked if she wanted to be a doctor when she grew up, she replied. "Yes, or a fireman!" After the ceremony, we all sipped Passover wine and ate sponge cake and macaroons. Friends and relatives said good-bye, and Larry drove me and our soundly sleeping son home to Clifton Park. We now could begin our life as a family.

I healed nicely and never needed surgery on the cyst. Outside of having to call the paramedics my second day home after I got my wedding ring stuck on my finger, things settled down to the new normal of having an infant. Over the years, Adam has had to celebrate many birthdays with Passover sponge cakes and macaroons instead of the traditional birthday cake. However, he and our family always enjoy the retelling of the Passover bris as much as the required retelling of our "sojourn from Egypt" at our Seders.

The Jewish World, April 10, 2014

Dayanu

Browsing recently at a Denver airport store on my way home to Orlando, I was greeted by the clerk. Exchanging pleasantries, I asked him how his day was going. "Counting the hours, ma'am. Just counting the hours."

"It can't be that bad," I replied.

"I am working a fifteen-hour shift in a newspaper stand in an airport," he said. "And this with a college degree. As I said, 'Just counting the hours.'"

Okay, so this young man was not living his dream. But all I could think of is that the clerk appeared to be the same age as a friend of mine who became a quadriplegic as a result of a freak accident twenty years earlier.

"Be grateful for what you have," I wanted to say to this total stranger. "Don't count the hours; count your blessings."

On Passover, we Jews celebrate the physical and spiritual redemption from slavery. Each year, we sing *Dayanu*, a song which lists the steps leading to our freedom. In it, we are reminded of our need—our responsibility—to be grateful for all G_d has given to us. "It would have been sufficient!" Dayanu!

Yes, it is sometimes difficult to be grateful. College degrees sometimes lead to menial job. Cars break down; toilets overflow; a bite into a hard candy results in a three-thousand-dollar dental bill. But as a dear friend said to me after I complained about a costly home repair, these are all First World problems.

In addition, in our highly commercial, secular world, it is sometimes difficult to be content with just enough. We are bombarded with advertisements promising us happiness if we only purchase a fancier car, a larger home, even a "natural organic" shampoo. We are exposed to all this noise on television, on billboards, on ever-targeted ads on the internet between our Facebook posts.

I am sure the Jews who escaped Egyptian slavery complained. Some of their *kvetching* is recorded in the Torah,—the first five books of the Jewish Holy Scripture. I can only imagine the grumblings that were not written down. "Manna that tastes like coconut cream pie again? For one night, can't it taste like my mother's matzoh ball soup?" Or: "Who put Moses in charge? We've been wandering this desert for forty years. The man can't find his way out of a paper bag!"

I was the child of parents who were on different ends of the "cup half full /cup half empty" continuum. I struggled as to whether my father's rose-colored view of the world was a better way to go than my mother's practical but less than optimistic outlook. Whereas my father was content with his life, my mother often compared herself and our lives to others, and she saw the grass as greener in the other's yard. "Comparison is the thief of joy," said Theodore Roosevelt. And also, in my eyes, the thief of gratitude.

When looking for property in Florida, Larry and I made the conscious decision to downsize. We chose a smaller home that, in line with most houses in the Sunshine State, had no basement and a fairly inaccessible, extremely hot attic. We purchased the property and all its furnishings in a community with a homeowners' association that takes care of our lawn and shrubbery. As a result, we divested ourselves of much of our belongings and started over. Once we unpacked—and gave another load of unneeded items to a local charity—we assured ourselves that we were never going back to having so much.

Despite my best intentions, however, I began to fall into my old habit of acquiring more than we need. The search for that one last item to complete our Florida home—a new outdoor seating set, a beach scene to place over the large sectional, updated lighting fixtures—was taking me away from where I wanted to be: grateful for what I have.

One day, while at a salon getting my hair cut, I saw a poster with the following affirmation: "Gratitude turns what we have into enough." And somehow that quote from Melody Beattie was the kick in the pants I needed.

Researching studies in positive psychology, I learned that those who are habitually grateful are significantly happier—and even healthier—than those who are not. One recommended method to enhance these feelings is by maintaining a gratitude diary in which one records on a regular basis three to five things for which one is grateful.

Using a beautiful floral-covered journal a dear friend had given me as a going away gift, I started 'counting my blessings' each night before I went to bed. Some entries were major milestones: "Sylvie walked across the living room floor!" Other day's reflections were more mundane: "Larry and I laughed our way through an awesome *Big Bang Theory* episode." No matter what the magnitude, I was ending my day focusing on the positive.

In the process, I have turned the focus from how many material possessions I have to how much goodness I have in my life. "Collect moments, not things" says a Hindu expression. The journal gives me the opportunity to capture those moments: savoring an Upstate New York apple, reading a book to my granddaughter, sitting on our lanai and viewing the wildlife in our pond, appreciating one more day of good health.

"If the only prayer you said in your whole life was thank you," wrote Meister Eckhart, "that would suffice." Or, in the word of the Passover Seder, *Dayanu! Chag Samaech!* Happy Passover!

The Jewish World, April 14, 2016

The Goldene Medinah

The history of the deadliest industrial disaster in the history of New York City is intertwined with my mother's family and in particular, my smart, generous, resourceful Great-Aunt Lil Osovitz Waldman.

My maternal family story began in Ragola, a *shtetl*—a small town with a large Jewish population—in the southeastern part of Lithuania. My grandmother Ethel's birth mother Channah married a Buck (first name unknown), a radical and a "free thinker." Buck's unorthodox views were too much for the religious Channah and her parents. Soon after the birth of their son Rafael, the marriage was dissolved. A few years later, Channah married Elihu Hirsch Osovitz. Rafael was soon joined by a half-brother Sam.

Five years later, Buck came to their home and took Rafael with him to America. Channah, heartbroken, died a few weeks later during childbirth. Channah's parents took Sam into their home. The infant Ethel—my future grandmother—was placed in a home of a wet nurse.

Three years later, Elihu fell in love with Faigah "Vichna" Levinson, the daughter of a prosperous couple in the baking and grocery business. Initially, Vichna's parents did not approve of their twenty-year-old daughter's marriage to a thirty-plus widower with two children. However, their union was a love match, a rarity in those days of arranged marriages.

Ethel adored her new mother. In fact, it was not until she was introduced to her maternal grandparents seven years later that Ethel realized that Vichna was her step-mother. During that visit, Ethel also learned that she had an older brother Sam in America.

Elihu was a pious man and a student of the Torah. Grandma Vichna was the breadwinner, working in her father's store. They shared an Eastern European style duplex with another family. Each side of the small wood building held one room with a curtain in the corner hiding a bed to provide the parents some privacy. The two families shared an outhouse.

By 1899, the couple had four more children sharing their one room house: Joe, Lil, Paul, and Rose. Fearful of the threat of pogroms, Elihu and Vichna insisted their oldest daughter cross the ocean by herself to *Die Goldene Medina*—the Golden Land—for a better life. At Ellis Island, fifteen-year-old Ethel was met by her brother Sam and her half-brother Rafael Buck. It was the first time she had met either sibling. Staying with distant cousins, Ethel got a job in an umbrella factory for three dollars a week.

Back in Ragola, behind that thin curtain, Vichna and Elihu conceived three more children: Bea, Ruth, and Morris. As the oldest girl living home, Lil was responsible for her younger siblings until she was sent to America when she was twelve years old to join Ethel.

The two sisters rented a room with a family of six children and four other boarders. Giving her age as fourteen, Lil obtained a job as a garment worker in a sweatshop in Greenwich Village. She viewed the location—the top floors of the crowded, airless Asch Building—as "a firetrap." To prevent workers from taking too many breaks or stealing, the owners locked the doors to the stairwells and exits.

Ethel, struggling and unhappy with her job, accepted her brother Sam's invitation to move in with him and his wife in Baltimore. Meanwhile, Paul, Joe, and Rose followed their older siblings to America.

When Paul encountered health problems working in the sweatshops, Lil relocated him and Joe to Burlington, Vermont. She also gave them money to purchase a wheelbarrow and enough second-hand items to peddle goods to Vermont farmers and their families. Initially traveling on foot and then on horse and wagon, the two brothers saved enough money to open a store in Alburgh, Vermont. This was the start of Pearl's Department Stores, a chain that grew to twenty-two stores in Vermont and Upstate New York.

Working in the factory on Washington Place, Lil proved to be a fast and efficient seamstress. When she demanded a raise, she was fired—a blessing in disguise. A week later, on March 25, 1911, the "firetrap"—the Triangle Shirtwaist Factory—was the scene of the deadliest industrial fire in New York City history. According to *Wikipedia*, one hundred and forty-six garment works died from the fire, smoke inhalation, or falling or jumping to their deaths. The tragedy led to legislation requiring improved factory safety standards and helped spur the growth of the International Ladies' Garment Workers' Union (ILGWU), which fought for better working conditions for sweatshop workers.

By that time, Elihu had died. Lil had saved $75 to pay for the remaining family members' ship passages. On April 11, 1911, an elegantly dressed Lil greeted Vichna (44), Bea (11), Morris (9), and Ruth (6) at Ellis Island. Lil rented an apartment on the Lower East Side of Manhattan for herself, Rose, and the four recent immigrants.

Lil continued to be the main breadwinner in the family. She obtained promotions as a seamstress in various factories specializing in blouses and dresses. She often made as much as $20 a week, a salary higher than most of the married men with whom she worked. Her hard work came with sacrifices. Lil attended night school, but after a hard day in the shop, she often fell asleep in class. As a result, she never spoke or wrote English proficiently, relying heavily on Yiddish her whole life.

Now that the entire Osovitz family was in America, Vichna now focused her efforts on making sure that her oldest daughter in Baltimore was married. She arranged a match between her Ethel and Joseph Cohen, a lonely tailor originally from Ragola who was sleeping on a cot in his sister's apartment. On January 14, 1912, Ethel and Joe were married in a large banquet hall filled with family and friends from the old country. Nine months and four days after the wedding, their son Eli—named after Elihu—was born. Five years later, they welcomed Frances—my future mother.

A few years later, with the entire Osovitz family finally settled in The Golden Land, Lil married Sam Waldman, a butcher. Lil worked alongside her husband in stores in New York State: initially in the city, then Long Island and St. Regis Falls. They finally settled permanently in the Syracuse area. The entire family remained close throughout their lives, as have their many descendants of the original nine siblings from Ragola, Lithuania. And all of us recognize and appreciate the strong role our Aunt Lil played in our history.

The Jewish World, March 16, 2017

The Four Cohen Kids

It is a hot day in late June. I wait impatiently on the front porch of our old Victorian house in our small upstate New York town. The blue sedan finally pulls into the driveway. My father climbs out from behind the wheel. As I skip down the steps and run across the yard. Dad opens the door on the passenger side. My mother holds a bundle wrapped in pink. I gaze in wonder upon a full head of dark brown hair and an infant's face crunched up and bright red from crying. "Meet your little sister Roberta Jessica," Mom said quietly.

That was my earliest memory. I was four years old, turning five and starting kindergarten three months later. I was thrilled to be a big sister.

I was probably the happiest of the Cohen family that day. My sister Laura, upon hearing before her thirteenth birthday that another child was on the way, immediately weighed in. "Why didn't you consult with me first?" she demanded. When told she was not part of the decision making process, she stated, "Well, if you think you have a built-in baby sitter, you have it all wrong!"

Jay, who was nine, only wanted a brother. When Dad woke him the morning of June 25 to tell him he had another sister, he groaned, pulled the covers over his head, and went back to sleep. I am not sure if he gave the newest addition another thought.

And I am not sure how happy my parents were when they realized that they were to be a family of six. Dad barely made enough money managing a small store to support a family of five, much less another child. Mom was thirty-six, looking forward to putting her youngest in full-day kindergarten and having a life without diapers and bottles.

But from the moment Bobbie came home (Roberta Jessica would forever more be saved for formal documents), I was fascinated. When my mother filled up the old bathinette with water to bathe her, I was right there beside her to help. When she needed to be pushed in the carriage, I wanted to be the one holding the handles. And when Bobbie needed casts on her legs to correct weak turned-in muscles, it was I who watched over her in her crib, which was set up next to the twin beds in my room.

I have heard stories about older children being jealous of their siblings when they came home from the hospital. Children who resorted to tantrums. Children who wanted to know when the baby was going back to the hospital. A five year old who rode her bike up and down her street crying, "Does anyone want a little girl? My parents don't love me anymore!" But I never remember being jealous. She was my little sister, my live baby doll.

If there were any difficulties between us, it was probably because everyone who met Bobbie immediately fell in love with her. She was always smiling, always happy, always easy going. This was in stark contrast to me—moody, anxious, and often fearful. Little Miss Sunshine could charm her way into everyone's heart, a direct contrast to my Little Miss Worrywart personality.

And Bobbie was beautiful. I was chubby, with thick glasses that covered my only good feature, my blue eyes. On the other hand, Bobbie had dark hair, high coloring, freckles sprinkled across her nose, and eyes that rivaled Elizabeth Taylor's.

As we grew up, Bobbie and I continued to be inseparable. She was always part of my parties, my sleepovers, my bike rides. In every one of the few pictures we have of our childhood, Bobbie is always front and center, her smile lighting up the world. Years later, when I asked my mother what it was like to have baby at thirty-six years old, she said, "I didn't raise her. You did!"

The four Cohen children are fortunate indeed. Whereas many of my friends have strained or non-existent relationships with their siblings and/or their spouses, we all have remained close—maybe even closer now that we all realize how life can change on a dime. When Bobbie called me ten years ago to share the devastating news that she had breast cancer, our initial thoughts were "This can't be happening to our little sister." But it was her "Little Miss Sunshine" attitude that got her through surgery, radiation, chemo, and her recovery. When Laura had a stroke this past winter, she often referred to Bobbie's spirit during her cancer ordeal and was determined to be as strong. She was.

One of our favorite pictures of the four Cohen kids was taken just

Tikkun Olam

before Laura graduated high school. We are sitting on a couch in our house in Keeseville—Jay siting on the arm rest, followed by Laura, Marilyn, and Bobbie. In a home with few family pictures, that particular one graced my parents' living room for the rest of their life. We siblings all kidded my parents and each other, wondering "This is the best we ever looked?"

The evening after my mother's funeral, we pulled out that picture. Bobbie's husband Emil posed us all on my family room couch with the four of us trying hard to duplicate our fifty-plus years-ago expression. Then we took a more straightforward one, without the silly grins.

We have continued the tradition. Each time we are together, whether it is at a bat mitzvah or a weekend reunion, we will line up—Jay, Laura, Marilyn, and Bobbie—snap a picture, and are grateful that the "Four Cohen Kids" are happy, healthy, and together again.

The Jewish World, June 3, 2017

Pressing Question?

When one is looking for a home in today's market, one of the featured perks is the laundry room. Multi-functioning washing machines and dryers, fancy cabinetry, shining stainless steel sinks, and granite countertops appear to make Wash Day a joy. What a contrast to the way my mother handled the laundry in Upstate New York in the 1950s!

In 1952, my family moved into a two-story house in Keeseville that had been built at the turn of the century. Compared to the 1200-hundred square-foot "box" in Potsdam, the four-bedroom Victorian with its large living and dining rooms, ancient but large kitchen, a large unfinished room off the kitchen that was immediately turned into the office, and three (!) porches must have felt like a castle.

Our laundry room, however, was a virtual dungeon. Out of necessity, the wringer washer had to be set up in the basement, a dark, damp room with dirt floors, old stone walls, and a small window that looked out to the crawl space under one of the porches. A single hanging bulb provided the only light.

With two adults, three children—including one in cloth diapers—and lots of company, my mother had plenty of laundry. The wonders of polyester and wash and wear were still several years away. Either clothes were dry cleaned or "put through the ringer." After a scare when my older sister Laura got her arm caught in the wringer mechanism, the old machine was replaced with a state-of-the-art top loading model. My mother considered herself in the lap of luxury.

Electric dryers had not yet found their way to Upstate New York, so all the wash had to be hung to dry. Mom carried the wet laundry up the steep basement stairs, walked through the kitchen and through the door to the back of the unfinished storage room. She opened a large window and hung the clothes from a thirty-foot long clothes line that operated on a pulley system. One end was attached to the house and the other end to an oak tree that marked the far right corner of our property.

During the good weather, sunshine and warm breezes would quickly dry the sheets, pillow cases, towels, diapers, shirts, pants, dresses, and underwear that hung ten feet above our backyard. If an unexpected rain storm came through, Mom would have to quickly pull everything off the line and hang them over every available chair and radiator to finish the process. During the long winter months, cold air poured into the unheated room as Mom, fingers red and raw, pinned the laundry to the line with the wooden pins. If the snow was too frequent, she resorted to hanging the laundry in the basement.

On the good days, Mom pulled the line of dry clothes toward the house, unpinned the items, and piled them into waiting laundry baskets. The cotton fabrics smelled like fresh air and sunshine but felt like stiff boards of wrinkled matzoh.

As a result, almost everything had to be ironed. Mom filled an empty soda bottle with water and stuck an aluminum and cork sprinkling head into the top. She lay out each item of clothing on the kitchen table, sprinkled the material well, rolled it up, and placed it in a laundry basket. She let all the dampened clothes sit awhile so the moisture would be well distributed. If she was afraid of mildew, she stuck the clothing into the large freezer chest that was housed in the shed until she found time to iron.

When she and the clothes were ready, Mom set up the ironing board in the kitchen, plugged in the iron, licked her index finger on her tongue, quickly touched its wet tip to the bottom of the iron to check the temperature, and then pressed the steaming metal plate into the fabric. Taking each damp, rolled piece out of the laundry basket, she ironed for hours while listening to the songs of Frank Sinatra, Patti Page, and Tennessee Ernie Ford on WEAV-AM radio out of Plattsburgh. The kitchen was filled with the sound of sizzling clothes and the smell of hot metal against the damp cotton.

The laundry increased with my sister's arrival three years after our move. By the time Bobbie was out of diapers, my parents had purchased a clothes dryer. My mother's lap of luxury had grown. Pink boxes of Dreft and plastic bottles of Clorox sat on a brown metal table between the two appliances, along with yellow bars of Fels Naphtha soap, stray buttons, and assorted socks missing their mates. The clothes line was only used on beautiful summer days as Mom still loved the smell of sunshine and fresh air on the sheets.

There was still a great deal to be ironed, so my mother gave her children pressing lessons at an early age. Starting with relatively easy handkerchiefs and pillow cases, we soon progressed to pants ("Make sure the seams are straight!") to shirts and blouses ("Start with the back and progress to the front and sleeves.") to dresses ("Lay the skirt on the ironing board, pushing the iron gently but firmly up to the waistband.").

I don't recall my father ever helping with laundry his entire life, but Larry has been by my soapy side since our apartment laundry room days. Once we moved into a house in Clifton Park, we set up an ironing board next to our washing machine and dryer in our basement/laundry area. To this day, he washes our bedding every week and does most of the laundry, including a weekly sheets and towel load. (Another reason I love him!)

Our "Yes! We're Retired!" Florida wardrobe doesn't require extensive pressing. No matter, at least twice a month, I pull out the steam iron and the twenty-year-old ironing board. I spread our shirts and blouses and pants and handkerchiefs one by one on the ironing board. I wet each item with distilled water from a plastic spray bottle, lick my index finger on my tongue, quickly touch its wet tip to the bottom of the iron to check the temperature, and then press the steaming metal plate into the fabric. I hear the familiar sizzle, and I breathe in the distinct aroma of cloth and water and heat and traces of laundry detergent. I am happy knowing that our clothes will be pressed and ready to wear—just like my mother taught me over sixty years ago.

The Jewish World July 20, 2017

Eye of the Beholder

While Larry and I were visiting friends in Tallahassee, Florida, recently, the four of us went to Wakulla Springs State Park. The 6,000 acre wildlife sanctuary offers a magical forty-five minute boat ride that takes its passengers past cypress groves, lovely springs, and a plethora of wildlife. Our tour guide, a delightful woman named Connie, navigated the boat through a narrow, shaded section of the ride and announced that this was the area in which *Creature of the Black Lagoon* was filmed in 1954.

I was all too familiar with the *Creature of the Black Lagoon.* When the movie arrived in Keeseville, New York, in 1955, my nine-year-old brother Jay had made plans to see it with a group of his friends. My mother, busy with a newborn, insisted that Jay take me, his five-year-old sister, along. We walked around the corner to the old theater in our small Upstate New York town, my brother grumbling all the way.

The first fifteen or so minutes were fine. The minute I saw the huge black amphibian-like creature emerge from the water, however, I became so frightened that I started screaming and crying. Jay had to leave his friends and popcorn behind to bring me home. "I told you I didn't want to take her with me!" my brother loudly complained to my mother. It was years before he took me to the movies with him again. The next horror movie I saw in its entirety was *Psycho*, Alfred Hitchcock's classic, when my college showed it on one of its movie nights.

I didn't fare any better with scary television shows. On November 11, 1960, my parents hosted a party for a group of their friends. My sister Laura and my brother Jay were supposed to be watching me in the family room while the adults congregated in the living and dining rooms. I insisted on staying awake, even when the *Twilight Zone* came on. The episode Rod Serling introduced that night was "Eye of the Beholder." The now-classic told the story of a young woman lying in a hospital bed, her head swathed in white bandages. She awaits the outcome of a surgical procedure performed by the State in a last-ditch attempt to make her look "normal." In the end, the doctor and nurses, who are only heard but not seen, remove the bandages to reveal a beautiful woman. As the medical team gasp with disappointment and revulsion, the camera moves to their twisted, grotesque faces. Beauty, it seemed, was in the eye of the beholder. In a scene reminiscent of what happened five years before in the movie theater, I screamed in fear and went running into the living room. The guests all trickled out as my parents tried to calm down their hysterical ten-year-old.

The end result was—well—"horror-able." I had nightmares for weeks. Laura and Jay were grounded for months. And it took years for me to watch the complete episode—ten months short of forty years, to be exact. On New Year's Eve, December 31, 1999, one of the cable stations offered a *Twilight Zone* marathon. The-episode-not-to be-named was shown between 11:30 pm and midnight. I watched it until the end, when the beautiful woman (played by Donna Douglas of later *Beverly Hillbillies* fame) was led out of the hospital by an equally handsome man to a place that accepted "ugly" people as their normal. It was only until the credits rolled did I turn the station to Dick Clark's show and watch the ball drop at Times Square to mark the new millennium.

For my entire life, I have avoided scary movies unless they are very old (the original versions of *Phantom of the Opera* and *Frankenstein*), very funny (*Little Shop of Horrors, Young Frankenstein*), or very well acted (*Silence of the Lambs, The Sixth Sense).*

Or made for children. Let's face it. Children's movies can be scary. Larry was so traumatized by the Wicked Witch of the West when he saw *The Wizard of Oz* as a four-year-old that he refused to watch the annual television broadcast for years. The evil queen in Disney's *Snow White* was as frightening to me when I was a child as Hannibal Lecter was to me as an adult. And the sea witch Ursula in *The Little Mermaid* still chills me to the bone when she appeared in her plump purple presence both on film and on the stage. But these animated antagonists who provided the tension in the children's classics didn't scare me enough to turn them off.

Once I became a parent, I shared my love for fairy tales with all their heroes and heroines and scary villains with my children Adam and

Julie. Thanks to Blockbuster and our VCR, we watched Dorothy, Snow White, Cinderella, Aladdin, and Ariel confront and conquer their demons again and again and again.

In 1991, when Adam and Julie were thirteen and ten respectively, *Beauty and the Beast* was released. It remains one of my favorite movies of all time, up there with *Casablanca* and *Schindler's List*. I was drawn to Belle's intelligence, her feminist streak, her strength. And I loved the Beast, with all his bluster and bellows, for his transformation into a loving, caring individual once he both received and gave the gift of love.

Julie told me this summer that my two-year-old granddaughter Sylvie loved the music from the movie, and I gladly shared my own enthusiasm with her. Together Sylvie and I listened to the sound track, watched some clips on YouTube, danced across the living room floor to the title song, and sang the songs on the way to her daycare. By the end of the summer, I had purchased the video and downloaded it to my laptop. Sylvie sat on my lap and watched mesmerized the entire length of the film.

When Larry and I returned to Colorado in October, however, Sylvie's attitude changed. "Little town, little quiet village…" was fine. But the minute the Beast arrived on the scene, Sylvie hid her face in her hands and said, "I no want to watch the Beast! I scared!" My showing her that short segment triggered a fear of all monsters, the ones in her closet, the ones under her bed, the ones hiding in the trees.

So the movie is off the radar for a while. Maybe by next summer, she will realize that Gaston, the handsome but chauvinistic and selfish oaf, is far more frightening than the considerate, loving Beast. Maybe she will have to wait five or ten or even forty years to watch the movie in its entirety. And maybe, as I did with Rod Serling's classic, she will realize like my heroine Belle that beauty is in the eye of the beholder.

The Jewish World January 4, 2018

Don't Hoard the Charmin'

The day before the Blizzard of 1993, local supermarkets were crowded with shoppers stocking up on milk and bread. According to my undoubtedly though unscientific research, the major run was on —toilet paper.

Friday morning, I tried unsuccessfully to get my neighbor Donna to go cross-country skiing.

"It's ideal conditions, Donna. And we could have the whole afternoon."

"Can't, Marilyn," Donna replied. "I have to go to the supermarket to buy toilet paper."

"Why are you giving up a perfect cross-country morning to purchase toilet paper?" I asked.

"I need to pick up a dozen rolls before the blizzard," Donna said. "I don't want my family to be stuck without toilet paper if we are socked in for a few days."

"A dozen rolls?" I said. "You won't go through twelve rolls of toilet paper in a month."

"You never can tell what will happen in a storm," she replied. "Maybe I'll see you at Price Chopper."

I resigned myself to cleaning house and running errands. Three hours later, I joined half the population of Clifton Park in the local supermarket to pick up my own family's emergency rations. Those included milk, Reese's peanut butter cups for my son, jelly beans for my daughter; ice cream for my husband; and kitty treats for Cuddles (heaven forbid my cat should be deprived during the storm).

Another one of my neighbors was in the dairy section grabbing his own gallon of one percent. I glanced in his cart and did a double take. At least a dozen rolls of toilet paper sat in between the eggs and some ground beef.

"You bought toilet paper!" I cried.

"Of course!" he said. "There's a storm coming."

"I guess every family has its 'necessities,'" I said, heading for checkout.

The lines were twenty-five people deep. People had their carts filled as if we were about to be overrun by an enemy horde. I took my place in the express line behind a young woman with her carton of milk, eggs, and chocolate chip cookies.

"Some storm we're supposed to get," I said. "The radio is predicting up to three feet of snow with winds up to thirty miles an hour."

"I just came in for tonight's dinner," she said. "People are going crazy. I saw one woman with at least a dozen rolls of toilet paper in her cart."

"It must have been my neighbor. Was she about five-foot-one with short blonde hair?"

"Nope. A tall brunette."

"Maybe people think that they will spend the entire weekend in the bathroom barricaded with toilet paper," I said.

Once I left the supermarket, I filled up the gas tank in my car as well as the gas can for the snow blower. At the hardware store, I purchased an extra flashlight and packages of "D" batteries. Before the children climbed off the school bus, I cooked up a huge pot of minestrone soup and some chicken and potatoes to tide us over in case the electricity went out.

By the time Larry pulled into the driveway, I was confident that I had successfully prepared our family for the storm. I told Larry about the day. I told him about the milk, the flashlights and batteries, the soup, the chicken, the gas. We were set.

"Sounds great," said Larry. "Did you pick up toilet paper?"

"What is this obsession the world has with toilet paper? We have three rolls downstairs in reserve," I said. "Besides, who says you need toilet paper during a storm?"

"You mean you didn't buy toilet paper?" demanded Larry. "What are we going to do if we wind up like Buffalo in 1977 and we can't get out of the house for three weeks?"

"We'll use Kleenex or newspapers!" I said. "WE don't need toilet paper."

"Kleenex will clog up the toilet, and the newspaper won't get through because of the storm."

"Look, Larry," I said. "If we get desperate, we could always walk to the Convenient Mart. It's only a mile away."

"Convenient Mart was out of toilet paper when I stopped for gas. The woman in line in front of me bought the last four rolls."

The ringing phone cut Larry off from any further discussion. It was my father calling from Florida.

"I heard you're getting a blizzard. Are you guys okay? You're not planning on going out, are you?"

"No, Dad, we're fine. We're staying home all day. I even bought extra flashlights and cooked chicken and potatoes to eat cold if the electricity goes out."

"Terrific," said my dad. "But, tell me, did you buy toilet paper?"

The next morning, hours before the storm hit, my husband ran out and bought six rolls of toilet paper. Yes, we survived the storm…at least in the bathroom.

The (Schenectady, New York) Sunday Gazette, March 21, 1993

Today I Am A Woman!

My education at Temple Beth Israel in Plattsburg, New York, was strong in Jewish history and traditions but weak in Hebrew. If I wanted to learn the language required to follow the service, I had to attend after-school classes twice during the week. This was difficult with its one-hour round trip from our home. The only alternative choice I had would be to prepare for a *bat mitzvah*, the Jewish female's coming-of-age ritual usually held on one's thirteenth birthday. Unfortunately, this was not something females did in the 1960s in Upstate New York.

Our father had grown up in New York City in the Depression. His *bar mitzvah* ceremony was celebrated with several boys in his Eastern Parkway synagogue, including the son of the shul's president. The honor conferred on this golden boy was his reading most of the Torah portion and the haftorah and giving a speech while the remaining *b'na mitzvot*—celebrants—were left with short prayers and shorter participation. The party consisted of some sponge cake and wine back at my father's house followed by playing sandlot baseball.

As a result of my father's experience, his son was to have everything denied the father. Jay's bar mitzvah was a huge celebration. Over one hundred and twenty people were invited to the service, including relatives we had never seen before and never saw again. Immediately following the service, my parents hosted a lovely reception at the Cumberland Hotel in Plattsburg. We all got new clothes for the party; I still can remember how special I felt wearing the "balloon" dress that was popular in 1961.

As was the tradition in our reform synagogue, my Jewish education officially ended at sixteen years old with a Sunday morning confirmation service. My class consisted of two other girls and me, none of who had bat mitzvahs. We recited prayers and gave speeches. Mine was on anti-Semitism. How in the world my teacher ever encouraged that topic and how I ever summarized its history in less than ten minutes I'll never know. But I proudly wore the white robe and mortar board cap and enjoyed the reception that followed. What I remember most was how one of my teachers gave my two classmates cards with cash gifts and completely ignored my presence. Not the sweetest memories to carry from my confirmation.

Despite the snub, I loved learning about Jewish history and traditions. I attended classes with the grade behind me and even helped out in the primary grade classrooms. Once I left for college at University at Albany, I attended services for Rosh Hashanah and Yom Kippur at Congregation Beth Emeth. I was not involved in Hillel, however, nor did I take any classes in Judaic Studies that were beginning to be offered by the college.

It was not until my children were born that my interest in studying Judaism returned. Over the years, I took some basic Hebrew and prayer book Hebrew classes so I could better follow the service. In the years I stayed home with my children, I seriously considered going back to school for a second master's in Jewish Studies, with an emphasis on Jewish women's studies. When time constraints ruled out classes, I began a self-tutorial, reading books by noted Jewish female writers, including Anzia Yezierska, Tillie Olsen, Cynthia Ozick, and Grace Paley. This all went on the back burner when I returned to a full-time teaching position in 1986.

In 1993, however, Flo Miller, one of Congregation Beth Shalom's teachers, suggested that I take a *Haftorah* class that summer with two other interested women. The four of us met each week around Flo's kitchen table to practice the Hebrew and learn the trope, or melody, for our portion that was read in conjunction with the Torah reading at every Saturday morning service.

By the end of the summer, each of us had chosen our own Haftorah for our adult bat mitzvah. I chose *Mishpatim*, the haftorah portion which fell that year on the week of my father's ninetieth birthday, a way to honor him. Coincidentally I was studying to reaffirm my link to Judaism at the age of forty-three—what would have been the thirtieth anniversary year of my own bat mitzvah. Over the next several months, my lunch hours at work consisted of hastily gobbled sandwiches and two practice readings of the Haftorah done in the privacy of my office. Once a week,

Flo would call me on the phone, and I would again read the portion to show her how well I had progressed. By winter, Flo, Rabbi Harry Levin and I decided that I would also read two Torah portions at the service.

My bat mitzvah, which was held on February 4, 1993, was not a huge affair. My parents and Larry's parents could not come from Florida, and my siblings were too spread out across the country. Many members of the synagogue attended, however, along with Larry's sisters and brothers-in-law plus a few close friends, I was proud to wear the *tallit*, the ritual prayer shawl that my mother-in-law had sent me from Florida. I read my portions and prayers with not too many noticeable errors. A Kiddish with challah, wine, and light refreshments followed. Then my family and friends went to a Chinese restaurant for a celebratory meal. Meanwhile, I recorded my Torah and Haftorah readings and sent the audiotape to my father for his birthday.

I would love to say that the experience resulted in further Torah and Haftorah readings at Congregation Beth Shalom. Unfortunately, learning Hebrew did not come easy to me. It never flowed off my tongue, and even though I enjoyed the musicality of the special musical notes, I continued to stumble over the Hebrew letters and vowels. My next experience reciting Haftorah for a service proved to be even more difficult for me than my initial experience, and I have not tried again. I continue to enjoy attending services and have high respect for the congregants who volunteer to read Haftorah and Torah portions. And through Jewish book clubs and my own independent reading, I will continue to study and appreciate the faith into which I was born into and now fully embrace by choice.

The Jewish World August 20, 2015

The Simcha That Almost Wasn't

Every simcha—celebration—is a cause for rejoicing. However, for the Cohen family, my niece's bat mitzvah in 2008 was an especially joyful occasion.

My sister Bobbie and her husband Emil started planning for their daughter Marissa's bat mitzvah soon after their rabbi had given them the December 5, 2009, date. Since everything had worked out well at their son Michael's bar mitzvah and party in 2005, they decided to have a similar service and a party at the same venue.

In May 2008, Bobbie received devastating news. While both her recent mammogram and ultrasound had come out normal, Bobbie insisted on following up with a dermatologist to biopsy a small cyst. Everyone, including her doctors, was shocked at the diagnosis: she had breast cancer.

Bobbie called me on her way home from the doctor. She sobbed; I tried to console her; she asked me to be at our parents' apartment that evening when she called them. My parents took the news especially hard. No one in our family had ever had breast cancer. How could this happen to their baby, their beautiful Bobbie? They told her that although they were too old to help her physically, they promised that they would be there for emotional support and would pray for her recovery.

We all were sad that evening, but that was the last time I heard my little sister cry. "There is a reason that everyone calls me Little Miss Sunshine," Bobbie told me a few days later. "I refuse to be anything but positive. I will beat this."

Over the next year, Bobbie underwent chemotherapy, a mastectomy, radiation, and reconstruction. The support of her husband, children, family and friends helped her. It was Bobbie's positive attitude, however, that got all of us through the stressful time. She cheerfully went to her "chemo parties" and continued her exercise regimen. She embraced wearing wigs, declaring, "My hair now looks good all the time." A few hours after having her mastectomy, she was on the phone chatting with family and friends. "I am on a road with a few bumps and turns, but it will straighten out again," she said. "Meanwhile, I have a bat mitzvah to plan."

In the middle of Bobbie's ordeal, my father's health began to deteriorate. Just before he died, Dad received a phone call from his oldest grandson and his wife to tell him that they were expecting their first child. "It will be a boy." Dad said. "Name him after me, but call him William, not Wilfred." He passed away a day later, November 20, 2008.

That left my mother dealing with Bobbie's illness and the loss of her husband of sixty-eight years. Mom was philosophical about being a widow. "Life is about change," she said. "Bill and I had a wonderful marriage, and I have to accept that he is gone." She spent quality time with her friends and family. She drew strength from both Bobbie's optimism and the positive reports from her 'baby's' cancer doctors.

By the following December, everyone was ready for the chance to celebrate. Friends and family came from New York, Arizona, Colorado, and California. The youngest guest was five-month-old William, or Will, my parents' newest great-grandchild. Before Friday night services, we all gathered in the top floor of the hotel to enjoy a huge Italian buffet set up by Bobbie and Emil.

The next morning, Marissa did a beautiful job leading the service and reading the Torah and haftorah. Bobbie, still sporting a wig, looked absolutely radiant. Emil just beamed with pride for his family, and Michael cheered on his sister. The party was a joy. My mother, not looking at all like a ninety-one-year-old widow, danced every hora and electric slide and cha-cha-cha. We took pictures of the entire Cohen family, with the four children and their spouses, the eight grand-children, and the seven great grandchildren. I was not the only one to shed tears of joy. "We were not only celebrating Marissa's bat mitzvah," my mother later reflected. "We were also celebrating Bobbie's good health."

Fourteen months later, my mother's health declined rapidly. As she approached her last days, Bobbie drove in from Boston to be by her side. My little sister, who had never taken a medical class in her life, turned out to the best nurse in the family. Bobbie took command and guided us in tending to her needs until Mom joined her beloved Bill on March 3, 2011.

In September 2015, Marissa left for college. Bobbie and Emil are enjoying their empty nest, often going into Boston on weekends to take advantage of all the city has to offer. They recently visited us in Florida. I pride myself in my energy and stamina, but I could barely keep up with the two of them as we explored Spaceship Earth and the World Showcase at Epcot; rode the Tower of Terror and watched fireworks at Hollywood Studios; and took pictures with 'Albert Einstein' and 'Steve Jobs' at Orlando's wax museum. And through it all, Bobbie sparkled and smiled. And I thank G-d every day that my little sister is healthy, active, and remains our Little Miss Sunshine.

The Jewish World, February 18, 2016

Generous Hearts

One of the joys of our lives has been our ability to have the time and luxury to travel. Larry and I have seen Macho Picchu shrouded in clouds.

We have savored coffee and pastries in Vienna, swum in luminous waters in Jamaica, and hiked trails in the Rocky Mountains. Along the way, we have met people who have briefly enriched our lives and, in some cases, have become dear friends.

It was on a trip to Greece, however, that we experienced an encounter that was so memorable, so unique, so generous, that it will always be considered one of the highlights of our travels.

In September 2014, Larry and I went to the Greek isle of Naxos with two couples that we had met through our trips to Jamaica. Peter and Margaret, who were from England, had recommended the island from their previous visits. We were joined by Linda and Rob, who came from Alberta, Canada.

We spent our first three days enjoying the beautiful beach across from our rented rooms above the owner's restaurant. In the evening, the six of us piled into our rented van and headed the three or four miles into town to eat at one of the many al fresco restaurants available in the town center.

Peter and Margaret had told us that the people of Naxos were known for their generosity, and we saw this at every meal the six of us shared. At breakfast, our hostess Anna always brought us "a gift" of donuts or pastries or biscuits with our eggs and toast. At dinner, along with the bill, our waiters brought out a complimentary treat —a glass of wine, some fresh fruit, a small parfait—that was always presented as "our gift to you for eating in our restaurant."

On the fourth day, Peter and Margaret suggested we take a day trip into the mountains to visit the Temple of Demeter, a site of ancient Greek ruins dating around 5300 BCE. We climbed up narrow paths to a lovely site overlooking green pastures and rolling hills on both sides.

After viewing the site and taking numerous pictures, we headed into the town of Filoti for lunch. We all dined on gyros, the national fast food of Greece, in an al fresco restaurant in a bustling town square.

After lunch, we walked through the town's quiet, narrow streets with marble steps leading up to residential homes and the town's Greek Orthodox church.

The outside of the church was in the iconic Greek style white walls with a large bell tower. Inside, we found a small room decorated with the icons, statues and similar symbols of Greek Orthodoxy. We each dropped a euro into a contribution basket, thanked the elderly gentleman who was serving as the church greeter, and started to leave.

The man stopped us, thanked us for our contribution, and in broken English, asked from where we were. We explained our nationalities—British, Canadian, American. After introducing himself as Georgio, he said, "Come, come see my home!" We followed him out of the church, up another flight of marble stairs, and in front of a lovely three story white building with the classic Greek doors.

Georgio led us into the first floor, where his wife was in the kitchen cooking at her stove. "Guests!" he said to her, and introduced his wife Athena. She greeted us as if having six strangers come into her home was an everyday occurrence, and joined Georgio on the tour. The living area was filled with ornate furniture, floors were covered in beautiful white marble, and walls were decorated with pictures of their parents, grandparents, and their two sons.

The second level, accessed through outdoor staircase, led to a bedroom off a balcony. The third level had another bedroom off another balcony that offered views of the church's bell tower as well as the surrounding mountains.

We posed for pictures with Athena and Georgio, thanked them, and began our leaving when Athena said, "Come! Come see our museum."

She grabbed a set of old fashioned keys and led us down the stairs to another white building with the ubiquitous blue doors.

Inside was a large room meticulously recreated by the local women's guild to look like a Greek home from the 1800s. A large table dominated the room, with walls covered with pictures of families from the 1800s, tapestries, and all sorts of embroidered dresses and linens. In the corner was a lovely canopied bed with embroidered nightgowns laid out as if someone was to slip into the warm comforters for the night. We felt as if we had stepped back two hundred years.

Again, we thanked her profusely and started to leave. "Wait!" she indicated, and pulled out of the cupboard a bottle of Ouzo, which she poured into small glasses and gave to each of us.

We all raised our glasses with shouts of *Yamas* and *Cheers* and *L'chaim!* She turned down our offer of euros for the museum. But when Peter pressed money in her hand and said, "For your church," she smiled and accepted it.

As we walked the short distance back into the center of town and our van, Peter and Margaret, seasoned travelers, commented that in all their years of seeing the world, never before had they encountered such generosity and openness.

"Can you imagine," Rob mused, "if I walked into my home with six strangers and said to Linda 'We have guests!'" The six of us left shaking our heads in awe. In a world filled with so much hatred and fear, we found a tiny town nestled in the hills of a Greek island filled with friendliness, warmth and two generous hearts.

The Jewish World, November 25, 2017

Never Forget

How does one comprehend the unfathomable? How does one grasp how six million Jewish lives were snuffed out by a world gone mad? For me, it was through the lives of Anne and Elie and Sophie and Pavel and many others. Thanks to brilliant writers, I have experienced the Holocaust through literature.

Neither of my parents spoke of lost relatives as their families had emigrated from Russia by the early 1900s. My initial in-depth exposure to the Shoah came from reading *The Diary of a Young Girl.* I was thirteen years old, the same age as Anne Frank when she started her journal. When I was worrying about acne and silly crushes while living in a small, upstate town, Anne was worried about having enough food and not being caught by the Nazis while hiding in an Amsterdam attic. Her words were prominently displayed on a poster on my bedroom wall throughout high school and college: "I keep my ideals, because in spite of everything I still believe that people are really good at heart." Her journal, found after she perished in Bergen-Belsen concentration camps, remains one of my most beloved books

As a first-year high school English teacher, I was assigned to teach Police State in Literature. It was a challenging course, made even more difficult for me as I was replacing a well-loved teacher who purportedly made *Brave New World* fun.

Instead, the students faced a young, idealist Jewish teacher who had been told to include in the curriculum *Night,* Elie Wiesel's memoir of his life in the Nazi concentration camps The following June, two of my students handed me their yearbook to autograph. They had drawn swastikas on my picture. Refusing to sign them, I sadly realized Wiesel's shattering tale had not impacted them as it had me.

Anne and Elie showed me the Holocaust through teenage eyes. *Sophie's Choice* forced me to see it through the eyes of a grieving parent. William Styron's novel depicted the story of a young mother who was forced by a camp doctor to make a heart-wrenching decision as she entered Auschwitz. She must choose which of her two children would die immediately in the gas chamber and which one would be allowed to live, albeit as a prisoner. Hoping her blue-eyed, blond-haired son had a better chance at survival, she sacrificed her daughter. I read the book when I myself was a mother of two young children. Reading about the grief and guilt that haunted Sophie for the rest of her short, tragic life broke my heart. Shortly after finishing the book, I woke up in the middle of the night screaming, "Don't take Julie! Don't take my daughter!" Reviews of the subsequent movie were outstanding, and Meryl Streep won an Academy Award for her performance as Sophie. I myself have never seen the film. It was hard enough for me to read the book.

In 1994, a collection of art and poetry provided a way for me to view the Holocaust through the art and poetry by Jewish children who lived—and perished—in Theresienstadt concentration camp. A line in a poem by Pavel Friedman (1921-1944) provided the book's name. "For seven weeks I've lived here/Penned up inside this ghetto/But I have found my people here./The dandelions call to me/And the white chestnut candles in the court,/Only *I never saw another butterfly.*" [Italics mine for emphasis] The butterfly became my symbol of the Holocaust. Even today, each time I see a butterfly, I am reminded of that young man standing behind a barbed wire fence wishing for freedom. In honor of Pavel and the six million, I wear a chain on my neck with two gold charms: a Jewish star and a butterfly.

In recent years, literature helped me explore the Holocaust from the perspective of those on the opposite side of those camp fences: people who eked out their lives in war-torn Europe during Hitler's reign. Kristin Hannah's novel *The Nightingale* followed the story of two sisters in Nazi-occupied France. The older sister Vianne desperately struggled to do whatever she could to keep herself, her daughter, and her friends—including a Jewish woman and her child—alive. The younger sister Isabelle risked her life to work for the Resistance. The description of physical and emotional deprivation experienced by those living through the four years of Nazi oppression gave me appreciation for the brutal, often deadly, conditions that were a fact of life for everyone—Jews and non-Jews—under Nazi rule.

Through a novel written by the daughter of a Holocaust survivor, I came to understand how experiences encountered in death camps often haunted not only the survivors but also their children. *The Speed of Light,* a novel by Schenectady native Elizabeth Rosner, tells the story of two adult children whose lives were shaped by their father's time in Auschwitz. While Paula tried to bring her father joy through her globe-trotting career as an opera singer, Julian, a scientist, lived as a secluded, highly structured recluse. "My father…carried his sadness with him, under his skin," Julien states. "It was mine now." How the siblings moved past their father's demons and redeem themselves was a fascinating read.

I am grateful that despite all that has already been written about the Holocaust, the topic still generates literature that gives us fresh perspectives regarding one the darkest periods in civilization. "Those who do not learn history are doomed to repeat it," wrote George Santayana. I will never fully understand the horrors endured by so many. But at least through the extensive amount of quality literature available, I can at least hope we can learn ways to assure "Never again."

The Jewish World, April 30, 2016

Golden Romances

What does *The Jewish World* have in common with the following six couples? All celebrated their golden anniversary, their fifty-year milestone in 2017.

Susie and Ed Goldberg met at a dance at The Laurels, a resort in the Catskills. Susie, who had just turned seventeen, came back to the room that she was sharing with a girlfriend and found several young men sprawled out asleep in the beds and couch of her hotel room. She called security to have them all thrown out. The story of the "Good Girl with Chutzpah" quickly spread through the guest grapevine. Ed was impressed. "If I ever go steady again, I want my girlfriend to be just like you," he said and then asked for her number.

After casually dating for eighteen months, the two started "going steady" once Ed was drafted into the army. When he got his orders to go to Vietnam, Ed proposed. Despite parental pressure to wait until he returned, Susie and Ed chose to have a small wedding at Temple Israel in New Rochelle, New York, a month before Ed shipped out. Fifty years later, Sue and Ed agree that many factors that constitute a great marriage: love, communication, empathy, patience, compromise, quality time with family, with friends, and especially as a couple.

"Bubbemeises"—tales from a Jewish grandmother—brought Hedy and Harvey Flechner together. They were just sixteen and seventeen when they started dating as freshmen at City University of New York. The first time she met him, Hedy's grandmother said he was an incarnation of her own late husband, Frank. "I've dreamed about this day," she told Hedy. "He's the man you're going to marry. Just finish your college degree first."

On their one-month anniversary, Harvey gave Hedy a red rose, a tradition he continues every month to this day. "When he was too poor to buy a rose, he'd steal one from a neighbor's garden," said Hedy. Six hundred and fifty roses later, they attribute their long marriage to carefully picking their battles and following Hedy's beloved grandmother's advice. "Never go to bed angry," she told the young couple. "It will take away the fun of being in bed together!" Smart woman, that bubbe!

A grandmother also had a hand in the Plass' marriage. While spending her summer on Far Rockaway on Long Island, Mickey was introduced by her girlfriend to "the cute boy who works at the penny arcade." After their first date, Grandma Spitz told the soon-to-be college freshman to finish her teaching degree before marrying Richard. "I told her I barely knew him," Mickey recalled, "but she insisted he was The One." They were married the summer after Mickey graduated college. The Plass' advice: Don't marry anyone with expectations to change them. "Why would you want to change someone you really love?" Mickey asked rhetorically.

Chris and Bernie Grossman met at a dance at Grinnell College at the beginning of her freshman year. Bernie, a junior was about to ask another girl to dance when Chris "got in the way." They dated while at college. As they both were from the Chicago area, they continued their relationship during school breaks and after Bernie graduated. They got engaged during the summer following her junior year. Chris took Jewish conversion classes through her senior year, and they were married the following summer after her graduation. Chris and Bernie follow the advice that Chris' parents offered at their fiftieth anniversary: "The secret of a long marriage is to always keep in mind that the little things that annoy you about your spouse are not that important in the grand scheme of things."

The Secans met on a blind date. Phyllis's sister-in-law and Joel's sister, who were friends, gave Phyllis' telephone number to Joel. Five months later, he finally made the call and invited Phyllis to lunch at Nathan's in Oceanside, Long Island. They had such a good time that lunch was followed by a movie, dinner, and a commitment for a date on Monday night. By Tuesday morning, Phyllis knew that this was "the love of her life." Ever since that night, Phyllis and Joel have built on their immediate mutual attraction by anticipating their partner's needs staying up when the other was down. Most importantly, they continue to find ways to keep the romance going. "Having a date night is a must,"

Phyllis said.

Betty and Steve Schoenberg were fixed up by their fathers, who knew each other through their jobs with the United States Postal Service. "Eighteen-year-old" Steve (he was actually twenty-one) asked sixteen-year-old Betty to join him on a boat ride on the Hudson River. Regarded at first as a passing summer romance, Betty and Steve continued to date that fall. "It was hard to say we didn't like each other when our own parents had set us up," recalled Betty. They got married after Betty's sophomore year at New York University. "A good marriage takes a great deal of patience," said Betty. And a good sense of humor—a VERY good sense of humor.

Six couples. Five decades of marriage times six. Eleven children and twenty-one grandchildren later, all have no regrets. Phyllis Secan summed up all the couple's life-long romances in her outlook on the future: "Our marriage just keeps getting better and better." Congratulations to the happy couples and *The Jewish World* on their fiftieth anniversary. May you all go from strength to strength.

The Jewish World, April 5, 2017

Big Wheels and Big Hills

Summer mornings on our neighborhood in Upstate New York during the 1980s were quiet—until eight o'clock. At that hour—designated by the parents to be late enough to 'start the engines'—the garage doors on almost every house opened simultaneously. A fleet of children, all sitting low on seats of their Big Wheels, flew down their driveways and began circling the 'track' that surrounded the grassy knoll in the middle of the cul-de-sac. The Daily Devon Court 500 was officially in session.

Biking had been part of life since I was a child. I spent hours riding a second-hand three-speed on rolling hills past apple orchards and Lake Champlain beaches. As adults Larry and I pedaled through the back roads of Albany County, me on that ancient three-speed and Larry on the bike he had ridden to deliver newspapers in Saratoga Springs.

Once our children graduated from Big Wheels to two-wheelers, the four of us took family outings on the Mohawk-Hudson Bike Trail.

When we turned forty, Larry and I traded in our relics for lighter, more efficient ten-speeds. Larry had to give up competitive running in 1996 due to an injury, and he began biking more frequently. He encouraged me to join him, and we pedaled our way around Southern Saratoga County.

Cycling became a social event. For a couple of years, a group from Congregation Beth Shalom in Clifton Park met on Sunday mornings in the synagogue parking lot for a ten to fifteen-mile circuit. Larry and I were enjoying our biking.

The length of our rides together increased: twenty miles, thirty miles at a clip. As a members of the Mohawk Hudson Wheelmen, we participated with fellow riders in metric half centuries, one in which I rode the sixty-two miles in honor of my sixty-second birthday. Larry completed a hundred miler with a more hardy friend.

Despite all my biking, I never was totally comfortable on hills.

While Larry gleefully viewed them as a challenge, I dreaded every long, steep incline. I usually made it with a great deal of effort. Once in a while, I had to resort to getting off the bike and pushing it to the top.

My fear of hills prevented me from taking advantage of all the biking trails near Julie and Sam's home in Summit County, Colorado. Larry had taken some rides with Sam, but I bowed out. On our visit in July 2012, however, I had several months of biking long distances in New York under my belt. Larry and I finally took Sam up on his offer to join him for what Sam billed as an easy, fairly flat twenty-mile ride around Lake Dillon.

"There is a *little* incline at the beginning of the trip," Sam explained while we adjusted our seat height on our rentals and snapped on our helmets, "but I am sure you two can handle it."

As Sam had promised, the first four miles on the bike trail, were fairly flat and straight. Then we arrived at the bottom of Swan Mountain. I craned my neck to view the bike lane that ran along a busy two-lane highway. The summit appeared to me to be five miles away,

"Sam, this is *not* a little incline," I said. "This is a *mountain*! How long is it? And what is the increase in elevation?"

"We go from 9100 to 10,200 feet, an eleven-hundred-foot ascent over about a mile," Sam conceded. "I promise we'll take it slow."

Within one half mile, I was huffing and puffing. And sweating. My shirt was stuck to my back; under my helmet, my hair was glued to my head; my socks were drenched. I even had sweat running out of my ear canals.

"I can't do it," I yelled to Larry and Sam, who were riding with little effort 200 yards in front of me. "I'm going to walk the rest of the way. I will meet you at the summit."

"Are you sure?" Larry asked. They barely waited for my breathless "Yes!" before they pedaled off and left me to push my bike to the top.

Fifteen minutes later, I met up with Larry and Sam at the Sapphire Point Overlook.

"I made it!" I said to Sam. "It's all downhill from here!"

Then I took a look down the trail. Whatever goes up must come down, but *this* down was a steep descent on a narrow, serpentine bike path crowded with more confident cyclists.

"What the heck, Sam?" I exclaimed. "I thought climbing up was bad, but I can't handle going down this obstacle course!"

"Sorry, Marilyn, but it's the only way back to our house without adding another ten miles," said Sam. "Just take it slow."

"Don't worry!" said Larry. "I'll be right behind you."

Larry's 'right-behind-you' promise lasted an even shorter time than Sam's 'we'll-take-it-slow' promise. Terrified and white knuckled, I kept hitting my brakes. Larry couldn't bike slowly enough to follow behind and had to go ahead. I prayed all the way down to the bottom, where I caught up with Larry and Sam for the second time that day.

The remaining miles were less dramatic. And by the end of our vacation, I had actually forgiven Sam.

Since my bike ride from hell, however, I haven't attempted a repeat in Colorado. These days, I love riding through my mountain-free community in Florida—elevation in the Orlando area peaks out at eighty-two feet above sea level. Big hills—like Devon Court's Big Wheels—are in my rear-view mirror. And that is fine with me.

The Jewish World, July 7, 2016

Bubbe Butt Paste

Soon after my daughter Julie and my son-in-law Sam told us they were expecting our first grandchild, my husband Larry and I discussed what grandparent name by which we each hoped to be called.

Larry determined quickly that he would be called Zayde. It was a family tradition, he stated. His father's father was Zayde Max, and his own father was Zayde Ernie to his seven grandchildren.

Choosing my name didn't come as easily. My friend Lynn, whose granddaughter lived in Israel, suggested the Hebrew moniker Saftah, but I didn't think that would work for our future grandchild, who would be living in the Rocky Mountains of Colorado at 9100 feet above sea level. The paternal grandmother, who had a four-year-old granddaughter, already had dibs on Nana. Additional members of the Grandmother Club told me about their sometimes unusual titles: MeeMaw, GG, G-Ma, CiCi, NayNay, Gemmy, and even (Graham) Cracker. Although Bubbe went well with Zayde, I dismissed it as too old fashioned. I pondered the numerous options over the next few months.

Larry and I were in Colorado the day Julie went into labor. While waiting for the Big Moment, we took a hike up to Rainbow Lake, a lovely spot a mile up the mountain near Julie and Sam's home. On the trail, we ran into another couple who, noticing Larry's Syracuse University hat, told us they were also from Central New York State. After chatting with them about the Orangemen's basketball team and the amount of snow that fell the past winter, Larry and I told them about our grandchild's imminent birth. They congratulated us, stating how much they themselves enjoyed being grandparents.

"What do they call you?" I asked the woman, whose name was—ironically—Julie.

"Grandma," she said. "I waited a long time for grandchildren, and I am proud to go by the standard name."

That sealed it for me. Meeting a Julie from Syracuse on a hike the day my grandchild was born was *b'shert*—meant to be. I would stick with the classic "Grandma."

Larry and I were introduced to our granddaughter, Sylvie Rose Massman, an hour after she was born. When I held her in my arms in the hospital room, I was in heaven. I was finally a grandma! I enjoyed every moment of that summer and the three visits over the next year.

By the time we returned to a rented condo for another Rocky Mountain summer just before her first birthday, Sylvie was talking. We secretly hoped that, along with her rapidly expanding vocabulary—*Dada, Mama, dog, bear, boo (*blueberries*), yesh,* and *dough (*no*)*—she would learn and say our names before we went back to Florida.

Happily, over the next six weeks, we spent many hours with Sylvie, not only with her parents but also without them as exceptionally willing babysitters. As she sat in her high chair eating her meals and snacks, I determinedly coached her.

"Sylvie," I said, touching her on the nose. "Dog," I said, pointing to Neva, who was waiting patiently with her tail thumping for the next dropped morsel. "Grandma!" I said, pointing to my chest. Sylvie would smile and laugh and offer me her smashed banana or mushed piece of challah. Nothing in her babbling, however, even came close to "Grandma."

Four days before we were to return to Florida, Sylvie and Larry were playing on the floor with her blocks. "Zayde!" Sylvie suddenly stated emphatically. Larry's face lit up like the Syracuse University scoreboard. She said it again—and again. From that moment, Zayde became her favorite word. She called out "Zayde!" the minute Larry walked into the room, and she yelled it out if he disappeared behind a closed door. Talk about melting a grandfather's heart!

As happy as I was for Zayde Larry, I was a little—well—make that *extremely* jealous. My efforts to hear Grandma—any version—intensified. "Grandma!" I said every chance I got. As the hour of our departure got closer, I became desperate and switched tactics. "Bubbe," I tried, deciding an old sounding name was better than no name at all.

The morning before we were to fly back to Florida, I babysat Sylvie while Julie and Sam were at work and Larry was returning the rental car. After her morning nap, I lay my granddaughter on the dressing table to change her diaper. She looked into my eyes and clearly said, "Bubbe!"

"Yes, Sylvie! Bubbe!" I cried. Sylvie had spoken, and I was going to be Bubbe! I was over the moon! I immediately shared the news with Larry. Sylvie said the magic word again after lunch and after her afternoon nap. When Sam returned home from work that evening, this Bubbe was bursting with joy.

"And she repeated this every time you changed her diaper?" Sam asked somewhat hesitantly.

"Every time!" I said. "She clearly said Bubbe!"

"I don't know how to tell you this, Marilyn," Sam said. "But she wasn't actually calling *you* Bubbe. It's her world for butt paste. She has had some diaper rash this past week, and—well—she likes to hold the closed tube after we finish applying it."

"Butt Paste!" Larry chortled. "She is calling you Butt Paste."

The day after we returned to Florida, Julie and Sylvie FaceTimed with us. The minute Sylvie saw our faces on the computer screen, she yelled out, "Zayde!"

"And look who is with me, Sylvie!" said Larry. "It's Bubbe Butt Paste!"

Sigh! I am sure she will be calling me Grandma soon. Until then, I will be happy to accept her smiles, her laughs, her waves, and her unconditional love—no matter what she calls me

The Jewish World, September 1, 2017

Adventures in Time Travel

In the early 1960s, *The Adventures of Rocky and Bullwinkle and Friends* television show included segments entitled "Peabody's Improbable Adventure." With the help of a time machine, "WABAC," (pronounced way-back) the dog genius and his adopted human son Sherman were whisked back to a moment in history, sometimes saving the day. As schools rev up to start the new year, I was thinking how much fun—and relevant—it would be if students could go back in time to a historic event, even as an observer. After I posted a request on Facebook, many shared with me of their own hypothetical adventures in time travel.

Steve Sconfienza, who has worked as both a pilot and a flight instructor, would take the way back machine to December 17, 1903, in Kitty Hawk, North Carolina. There he would see first-hand the moment that Orville and Wilber Wright became the first people to accomplish powered flight. For centuries, many had always believed that human beings could find a way to fly. On that historic day, the two brothers, whose interest in flight had been sparked by a rubber band driven toy helicopter their father had given them twenty-five years earlier, flew the first successful airplane. "Although not the first to build and fly experimental aircraft," states Wikipedia, "the Wright brothers were the first to invent aircraft controls that made fixed-wing powered flight possible." Steve, a flier since he was sixteen years old, viewed the Wright Brothers' accomplishment as "a real triumph of humanity's reach for knowledge."

Sherri Mackey, a woman whose faith has shaped her own strong voice regarding social issues, stated she would go back to the early twentieth century's suffrage movement and be present for the certification of the ratification of the Nineteenth Amendment on August 26, 1920. Sherri reflects, "I can only imagine the joy for women that had fought hard for the right to vote." Sherri continues to work to ensure that folks with alternative agendas do not somehow dilute voting rights. "We must teach our daughters to embrace their equality," she stated, "and to protect and defend their equal rights just as diligently."

Sharon McLelland dreams of being at Pimlico Race Course in Baltimore, Maryland, on November 1, 1938, to witness firsthand Seabiscuit's victory over War Admiral. At what was billed as the "Match of the Century," Seabiscuit, described in Wikipedia as "undersized, knobby kneed, and given to sleeping and eating for long periods" was the underdog who became an unlikely champion. The horse was regarded as a symbol of hope in a country that was fighting its way out of the Great Depression. Sharon, who once lived near Pimlico, now lives near Saratoga Springs, considered by many to be "the queen of the tracks." How fitting for a woman who as a child had pictures of Secretariat on her bedroom walls.

I would take Mr. Peabody's machine to the debut of *West Side Story* on Broadway on September 26, 1957. Oh, how I wish I were sitting third-row center when the world was introduced to this American classic! Seven years old and three hundred miles away, I listened to the cast recording my father had purchased for me the week Leonard Bernstein's masterpiece debuted. For years, I played and replayed the 78 rpm—"Something's Coming," "Maria," and the absolutely stunning duet "Tonight"—until I wore out the grooves. If I could be "Somewhere," it would be at the Winter Gardens Theater that opening night.

After decades of speculation as to who would finally accomplish the track and field milestone, Roger Bannister became the first person to run the sub-four-minute mile at the Iffley Road Track in Oxford, England, on May 6, 1954. My husband Larry became interested in track and field in junior high and read numerous articles and accounts and the runner's 1955 autobiographical account, *The Four Minute Mile*. As he has shared with me soon after we met, Larry wished he had been there when Bannister crossed the finish line with a time of 3:59:4. For his efforts, Bannister was named the first-ever *Sports Illustrated* Sportsman of the Year. Just recently, Larry found on YouTube a grainy black and white video of the race with Dr. Bannister himself doing the voice-over. Larry was ecstatic. Fittingly, a copy of Bannister's book still sits on our bookshelf.

Rabbi Beverly Magidson would be transported to Jerusalem after Israel's victory during the 1967 Six-Day War. She would like to have stood at the Kotel when the Western Wall came under Israeli control. Late Prime Minister Yitzchak Rabin described it in a speech to Knesset in 1995: "Nobody staged that moment. Nobody planned it in advance. Nobody prepared it and nobody was prepared for it; it was as if Providence had directed the whole thing: the paratroopers weeping—loudly and in pain—over their comrades who had fallen along the way, the words of the Kaddish prayer heard by Western Wall's stones after nineteen years of silence, tears of mourning, shouts of joy, and the singing of *Hatikvah* [Israel's national anthem]."At the time of the war, Beverly was in high school and only vaguely aware of the Kotel's significance. However, in 1969 she stood at the wall for the first time. It was a quiet moment in the late evening, and it was a powerful spiritual experience.

When Woodstock, the iconic four-day rock/love fest, took place in August 1969, Barbara Peterson was a 29-year-old stay-at-home mother with three young children. At the time, she was married to a controlling man who thought hippies were disgusting druggies, and she was a dutiful, strait-laced wife. This all changed in 1972, when Barbara divorced her husband, went to rock concerts, and became liberated. "That is when I truly regretted missing that historic moment in cultural history," said Barbara. She has thought about going back to the planned fiftieth anniversary event, but she said it wouldn't be the same.

The Wright Brothers. Women's right to vote. Seabiscuit. Bannister's sub-four-minute mile. *West Side Story*. The Western Wall. Woodstock. Historical moments that have resonated and remain important in individual lives. As the new school year begins, may our children's teachers help students find their own iconic moments in history.

The Jewish World, August 4, 2016

The Shul at 10,200 Feet

While in Colorado during the summer of 2016, my husband Larry and I visited the town of Leadville during its Boom Day Festival, a celebration of the Old West. The streets were filled with gunslingers, burro races, mining skill contests, and over one hundred food and craft booths. We got ice cream cones and wandered down West Fourth Street, past a mining skills contest, where brawny men and women competed to see how many pounds of rock one could pile into a truck. And just down the street, we found Temple Israel Foundation, a museum dedicated to a thriving Jewish community that existed in this Rocky Mountain city over one hundred and twenty years ago.

Leadville, located at 10,200 feet above sea level, is the highest incorporated city and the second highest incorporated municipality in the United States. The town's boom started in the late 1870s with the discovery of silver, resulting in an influx of migrants to this small mountain town. At its peak, the population of Leadville grew to approximately 30,000 residents.

Among the many groups of people attracted to the minefields in the high Rockies was a group of Jewish immigrants who migrated to the West and Colorado. Representing only 1% of Leadville's population, the three to four hundred Jews came to Leadville for the same reasons as their non-Jewish counterparts: to improve their social and economic status, to find adventure, even to reinvent themselves. As early as 1879, Rosh Hashanah services were held in the local opera house, and The Hebrew Benevolent Society acquired a cemetery for Leadville Jews in 1880. Soon after, the Jewish community built a synagogue and held its first service on September 19, 1884, the first day of Rosh Hashanah 5645.

For the next thirty-eight years, Temple Israel served a surprisingly large and active Jewish community. As a booming mining town,

Leadville's residents had ample opportunities to spend their earnings on clothing and household goods, liquor, sex, and gambling. Leadville Jews provided services in all these areas in the forms of dry goods stores, wholesale liquor and tobacco businesses, saloons, gambling houses, opera houses, and even brothels.

More well-known members of Temple Israel included David May, the founder of May department stores; Benjamin Guggenheim, heir to the famous family's fortune made in Colorado mines; and Leopold H. Guldman, philanthropist and founder of Denver's Golden Eagle Dry Goods Company. Despite its seemingly remote location, Leadville was a modern industrial city. Jewish dry goods merchants offered the latest European fashions to the ladies, and the better off gentlemen often sported diamond studs to accent their wardrobe.

By the first decade of the twentieth century, the boom was over, and the town's Jewish population began to decline. In 1912, the last recorded event, a wedding, took place.

From 1914 through 1937, the synagogue sat shuttered and unused. The synagogue was converted into a single-family residence, and the building took on various non-religious functions, the last as four rental apartments.

In 1983, Bill Korn, a New York City native, relocated from Boulder to Leadville to take advantage of low real estate prices and proximity to excellent skiing. He purchased and was in the process of renovating several properties when he learned of the former synagogue and its overgrown cemetery. Motivated by his own German Reform Judaism roots and his belief in Martin Buber's command, "If not you, then who? If not now, then when?" he explored ways to obtain both properties.

In 1987, the Temple Israel Foundation was incorporated "to acquire, historically rehabilitate, and maintain" the building, which was purchased in 1992.

For the next several years, Korn used the four apartment rental incomes to pay off the mortgage. The Foundation obtained a grant from the Colorado Historic Fund. Finally, ninety years after the temple shut its doors, renovations began to return the building to its former glory.

Meanwhile, the Denver chapter of B'nai Brith led volunteer efforts each June to maintain the cemetery grounds and replace markers. The cemetery was reconsecrated and began holding Jewish burials again in

2001.

In 2012, a permanent exhibition opened which documents pioneer Jewish life with a collection of artifacts about Leadville, its resident Jews, Temple Israel as a synagogue, and life in a mining town in the 1880s and 1890s.

While not providing regular services, the building, with its Torah and bima in front of the rows of pews, is now open for special events. Today, according to Korn, there are approximately 80 to 100 Jewish people in the entire county.

Bill Korn oversees the museum. From May through October, two full-time staff members work as both guides and researchers.

Over 3200 people visit the museum each year, said Korn. They come not only from surrounding Colorado towns but also from all over the United States and even Israel. Korn said his most special guest was Leopold H. Guldman's, granddaughter whose emotional response to the museum brought tears to Korn's eyes.

Larry and I now belong to a synagogue in Kissimmee, Florida, elevation 49 feet above sea level. Throughout the High Holy Days, we remember the lovely synagogue situated in the highest incorporated city in America. We continue to think about Bill Korn and his generous efforts to bring that synagogue to life for future generations. And we will always remember the long-ago Jewish congregation in Leadville celebrating Jewish life high in the Rocky Mountains.

The Jewish World, September 29, 2016

Collect Memories, Not Things

After Larry and I had been retired for four years, we seriously began thinking of selling our house and downsizing. We were not sure of the location. A smaller place in Clifton Park? Colorado to be closer to our children? Florida to get out of the cold? No matter where we landed, we knew we had to get rid of all the stuff that we were not going to take with us.

When my parents sold their house of thirty-one years in 1981, they found an easy way to avoid having to make decisions as to what to keep and what to toss. They loaded everything on which they couldn't decide into a rented U-Haul and told us to pick it up. My parents' rationale was that they weren't sure what was valuable and what should be tossed. They thought that we could be more objective as we cleaned it out. Larry and I drove with the children to my parents' home at Five Vine Street, loaded up a rented U-Haul, and Larry drove the van to our house. We then transferred all their treasures into our garage.

When we opened up the boxes, we found some items of either monetary or sentimental value: French casseroles with bird designs, some vases, a painting of a little girl with a kitty that had hung in their living room. For the most part, however, it was just stuff that they didn't want: smelly books, dishes from Dreft detergent boxes, steak knives given away with a fill-up from the local gas station, old cameras and radios. Once we unloaded all their stuff in the garage, there was no room for a car. Fortunately, our synagogue had a garage sale soon after we brought the filled van down from Keeseville. With some liberal pruning, I donated what we didn't throw out to the fundraising event.

The U-Haul trick wasn't going to work on our children. Our daughter and her husband lived in a small home in Colorado, and our son had an 800-square-foot apartment four flights up in the middle of San Francisco. Besides, we have told them the U-Haul story too many times for them to fall for it like we did.

Fortunately, while we were going through the process of divesting ourselves of thirty-eight years of home ownership, I read Marie Kondo's international best-seller, *The Life-Changing Magic of Tidying Up.* One of the major points in the book was the advice, "Get rid of anything that doesn't spark joy." We certainly had plenty of non-sparking-joy stuff. Some went into the recycling or garbage receptacles. I had no problem tossing my six years of back issues of *Hadassah* magazine. Larry did the same with his *Sports Illustrated* magazines, several pairs of old running shoes, and old running gear.

Following the advice of experts, Larry and I found homes for items we couldn't toss but no longer wanted. I gave away several cookbooks I had purchased with good intentions of learning how to make fancy appetizers, homemade pasta, and sacher tortes. Little used kitchen appliances and duplicate pie tins, tea pots, and sauce pans were donated to the local thrift shop. The stereo set with the turntable we hadn't used for twenty years found a second home in a friend's house, as did the stationary bike and the weight machine that would not fit into our planned smaller living spaces.

Our family, many of who lived near-by, took or purchased items that we would not need in our downsized life: the pool table, Larry's mother's silver, my grandfather's sewing machine. The two hundred or so unread books I had accumulated over numerous library book sales were given back to the library or to a nursing home. I downloaded my CD collection onto my computer and an external hard drive. Then the CDs themselves—Barbra Streisand, innumerable cast recordings of Broadway shows and sound tracks of movies, Bob Marley and Linda Ronstadt—were happily taken by friends.

I found decisions on items with emotional attachments more difficult. How could I part with the two Mexican dolls my father bought for me in Montreal when I was eight years old? I kept them! What about the dress I was wearing the night I met Larry? I had the picture of that night many years before, so the dress went to the thrift shop.

A file drawer was stuffed with my children's art work and projects from nursery school through high school, and a trunk tucked in the basement had their favorite baby blankets, some special clothing, and Adam's Superman doll that Julie "gave" him when she came home from the hospital.

Following the advice of the experts, I took pictures and texted them to our children. They asked for some things, but for the most part told me to toss them. I took one last look, took a few more pictures, and did what they requested.

Collect memories, not things. It was time to start over with a new home, a new life, new things to spark joy.

The Jewish World, July 9, 2015

If You Listen...

*When you talk, you are only repeating what you already know.
But if you listen, you may learn something new.*
             Dalai Lama XIV

So many stories if we just listen. Sitting next to someone on a plane, we often stick earbuds in our ears to make sure they don't prattle on about nothing. But sometimes there is much to be learned from hearing—and genuinely listening—to what others have to say.

Some of us are experts at listening. Lou, a friend and former co-worker, not only hears what the person is saying but engages his entire body: he leans forward, plants his chin in his hands and his elbows on his knees and looks the speaker in the eye. He nods in agreement. You know he cares about what is being said.

I think of Lou, and I want to emulate him. I am as guilty as anyone, often not actually paying attention.

How many times have I sat through a rabbi's *dracha*—sermon—and spent too much of my time checking my watch? Even when I have signed up for a lecture sponsored by my community's book circle, I often find myself thinking about what I need to do later that day rather than focusing on the topic being discussed. I have missed much by not being more mindful.

Our failure to focus often carries into our daily conversations. We often are not listening to what the person is saying but rather waiting for the moment to express our own "pearls of wisdom." And what is worse, what we want to say takes the conversation in a different direction. "That's great," we comment. "That reminds me of the time **I**...." Note the emphasis is on the word "I." To quote John Wayne, we are "short on ears and long on mouth."

We can learn from Lou and other good listeners. Young adult

author Sarah Desson describes them well: "They don't jump in on your sentences, saving you from actually finishing them, or talk over you, allowing what you do manage to get out to be lost or altered in transit. Instead, they wait, so you have to keep going."

How much richer our lives can be if we allow the speaker to continue talking.

In October 2016, Larry and I spent time with a group of friends in Key West, Florida. Before the trip, Larry had played pickleball with several people in the group, and we both had shared time around the pool and eaten lunch together. But being together for a week gave us more time to learn about each other's lives.

Stories abounded. One woman had contracted polio when she was six, just months before the polio vaccine had come out. An attractive woman who was visiting from England had become an actress in her sixties and is a regular on a British medical drama. A couple's son had left his career as a graphic designer behind and became a tattoo artist. Several in the group had served in the military and regaled us with their stories about their experiences in basic training, in fighter planes or in submarines. Again and again, I thought to myself, "Who knew?"

Four days into our trip, Larry said to me, "I love hearing everyone's stories!" As I did. So many stories, so much to learn. And as my friend Lynn tells me about her own life, "You can't make this stuff up!"

Through my writing, I have been happily gathering stories and sharing them with my readers. My friend's son, whom we have known since childhood, is now a rabbi in New Orleans. A member of our synagogue, a Holocaust survivor, was instrumental in the construction of our synagogue in Kissimmee. ("I saw a synagogue burn," said Harry, "and I was determined to build another one.") A thirty-nine-year-old resident of the Daughters of Sarah Nursing Home, paralyzed from the neck down in a freak motorcycle accident when he was sixteen, strives to wake up each morning with a smile on his face. Each has a story to tell, and we can all learn by listening.

At one of the meetings of my writer's group, one of the members shared a poignant story she had written about a woman she met twenty years earlier on a train stuck outside of Washington, DC. The writer—who was *not* wearing earbuds to block out conversations with strangers—learned that the woman was recently married to her childhood sweetheart. A month before the wedding, he was in a terrible accident and suffered traumatic brain injury. Despite warnings from friends and family to back out of the wedding, the young woman realized her vow to love one another through sickness and health had been sealed before the ceremony. By the time she finished reading her story, many of us were in tears. "How did you learn so much about a complete stranger?" we asked.

"I don't know," she answered. "She talked, I listened, and I remembered." Good advice for all of us.

The Jewish World, November 10, 2016

NOT the Party of the Century

One December, my friend Susie called me about the upcoming New Year's Eve party she was hosting at her home.

"I am so stressed!" Susie told me. "I don't know if I ordered enough food. And I think my dining room table is too small for this many people."

"Susie, take a deep breath," I reassured her. "Everyone who was invited appreciates your hosting, and it will all go well."

"What if they don't like the desserts I ordered?" Susie continued. "And I forgot the plastic champagne glasses, so I have to make another trip to Publix. Oy!"

Planning a *simcha*—a celebration—whether it be a dinner at one's home or a bar/bat mitzvah or wedding—is always stressful. And much of the angst comes from our need to make the occasion perfect.

My mother didn't seem to stress when she had huge family gatherings. We were used to fifteen to twenty around the table when our relatives came to our house in Upstate New York for a Sunday get-together. Our oak table expanded to fit as many chairs and high chairs that were necessary. All the relatives brought something—Cousin Shirley's noodle pudding, Uncle Paul's pickles, Aunt Rose's apple cake. Looking back, what amazed me the most was that Mom not only served lunch but also served the left-overs to everyone a few hours later for dinner.

When my parents purchased the cottage on Lake Champlain, the parties continued. The guests poured out onto the lawn and, between lunch and dinner, into the lake for a swim or boat ride. By this time, Mom had three grown daughters to help share in the preparations.

To be honest, it upset me that she would usually plan the gathering when my husband Larry and I were visiting with our two children. I would spend at least one day helping her prepare all the food. The day of the party, I was chief cook and bottle washer. "Isn't it wonderful to have

Marilyn here to help you?" Aunt Dot would comment as she helped herself to second piece of apple cake. I wanted to throw the towel at her and make *her* dry the dishes. Fortunately, along with teaching me how to cook, my mother had also taught me manners.

My mother-in-law Doris was the master dinner-for-the-crowd planner. Weeks before we celebrated any major Jewish holiday, my "second mom" would call me with updates on her progress. "I made the brisket and the chicken soup. They're in the downstairs freezer," she would report proudly. "And I am now in the middle of making the chopped liver."

All of us guests brought a side dish, but Doris was confident that the food items she had made were the tastiest ones on the table. We left with full stomachs and fuller doggy bags so we could enjoy her cooking the next day.

After Larry's mother passed away in 1994, we deeply missed her legendary holiday meals. Fortunately, the Shapiro family had all inherited the same love for company, cooking, and baking. Her children took turns hosting dinners, with every guest contributing his or her specialty—Carole's broccoli casserole, our cousin's Freya's tabbouleh salad, Anita's rugeluch, my mandel bread, Nelson's box of Jelly Belly jelly beans. Weather permitting, my brothers-in-law grilled chicken or beef. No one went home hungry or unhappy.

As my mother approached her eighties, she relinquished her command of the kitchen to the next generation. Our family gatherings continued around the old oak table at the cottage on Lake Champlain. Now, however, her daughters and daughter-in-law took over all the preparations. Once my parents moved to an independent living place close to me, my home often became party central when out-of-town friends and relatives came to visit.

For many years, my concerns mirrored Susie's. I was afraid that I wouldn't have enough food. That the mashed potatoes would turn out the consistency of glue. That I would burn the candied carrots or underbake the pumpkin bread. I worried that my house wouldn't fit everyone, or it would rain and people couldn't escape outside.

Somewhere along the line, however, I began to relax as I developed what I call the "Marylou Whitney" philosophy. Marylou Whitney is a philanthropist and prominent socialite known for her huge, elaborate parties she held in Saratoga Springs during the racing season. Every time I had a party, I would keep saying to myself, "Marilyn, you are not Marylou Whitney, and this isn't the party of the century. It will be fine."

So when I had my crowd of twenty-five to thirty people for one of the Jewish holidays or a large group of friends over for dinner, I built on my past experiences. I learned from my mother-in-law to prepare as much as I could in advance. I learned from years of being both a guest and a host that most invitees' initial comment after they said, "We would *love* to come!" was "What can we bring?" And I learned from my mother that houses and tables stretch nicely when filled with the combination of delicious food and lots of people you love.

I carried the "Marylou Whitney" philosophy over to my children's bar and bat mitzvahs and my daughter's wedding reception. The people who loved us would be happy to share the day. Any kvetchers (complainers) faced the possibility of being scratched off the guest list for our next party.

And Susie's party? It was fun! The nine couples shared chopped liver, deli trays, and super rich chocolate brownies. And wine. Lots of wine. It was a great start to the New Year.

The Jewish World, February 16, 2017

"Let's RummiKub!"

"Let's RummiKub!" read the email blast from my friend Hedy. She and her husband Harvey loved playing the game, and she decided to start a club in our community.

RummiKub! The last time I had played the popular tiled game was with my mother, Frances Cohen, before she passed away in 2011. She had played weekly with a group of women friends when she lived in Florida. When she and my father moved to an independent living community four miles from our home in Upstate New York, her game set came with her. Within a month, she had found another RummiKub group. She loved the socializing, challenging her mind—and winning. My mother was exceptionally good at finding ways to dispose of all her tiles by adding to accepted combinations of straights and matching numbers on the game table.

Before cell phones, before computers, adults and children played games—card games, board games—with *real* people. My siblings and I gathered around the old oak dining room table and played Old Maid, Go Fish, War, and—my favorite—Gin Rummy. We also enjoyed beating each other at board game as Chutes and Ladders and Candy Land gave way to Clue, Scrabble, and Monopoly.

Once my parents purchased their cottage on Lake Champlain in 1966, board games filled many empty hours. When bad weather kept us inside, my mother would pull out a deck of cards or the Scrabble set to keep us—and eventually—the grandchildren busy. One Monopoly game was good for an entire rainy afternoon.

In college, my friends and I would gather a few times a week for pinochle. We would sit around the circular table in the common area outside our suites in Paine Hall at University at Albany. I left college and pinochle behind, but games were still in the cards for me.

In May 1973, I met my future husband Larry's family. Within minutes, his Bubbe Rose challenged me to a game of gin rummy. She let me win almost every time over the next four months. Once Larry and I were engaged, the gloves were off. I rarely won again.

Playing card and board games together have always been part of our marriage—with varying levels of success. In the months following our September 1974 wedding, we often played Mille Bournes, a French card game. I soon quit as Larry always won. After we had children, we often played Scrabble on snowy nights while they slept. Larry once put down four tiles to spell "oije." When I challenged him, he said it was a popular word in New Jersey as in "I had the *oije* to go out for a hamburger." I *urged* him to remove the tiles. He still won the game.

Yahtzee is hands down our long-time favorite. The game, which requires the players to roll five die three times each turn to get one of the eleven required combinations is part chance, part luck. Larry usually wins. (Do you see the pattern here?) No matter. I pack Yahtzee into my suitcase every time we go on vacation. If the need arises to fill in some free time, we can resort to an activity *together*, infinitely better than burying our heads into computers and playing Solitaire (me) or Angry Birds (Larry).

We also played games with our children. By age four, Julie was so good at Memory that Larry was the only one who enjoyed losing to her. Clue, Uno and Sorry! dominated our lives for many years. Adam and Julie pulled out Monopoly to play with friends and each other until the sets literally fell apart.

The tradition continues. Larry and I joined Julie and her husband Sam for an overnight stay in a hut buried in the woods at ten thousand feet in the Rockies. The hut had no running water, a wood stove, and an outdoor bathroom, but it had Monopoly. Julie gleefully proclaimed victory after a two-hour marathon game. Just this past Thanksgiving, I taught Adam gin rummy. After the first hand he won the next four games against me. (Do you *now* see the pattern?)

When I lived in Upstate New York, several of my friends were in Mah Jongg groups. "Do you Mahj?" they would ask. No, I didn't. My mother-in-law Doris had played, but I didn't have a "Clue" as to what the game entailed.

It wasn't until I moved to Florida and was asked again if I "Mahjed" did I give the ancient Chinese game a try. I loved it! It had, in my mind, the best elements of every game I had had ever loved: Go Fish, Gin

Rummy, Yahtzee, and RummiKub. As my sister-in-law inherited her mother's set, I quickly purchased my own. I even brought the set with me—along with Yahtzee—on a recent cruise. I played with friends four mornings while at sea, so it was worth schlepping the three-pound tote on board.

Meanwhile, Larry and I took Hedy up on her offer. About forty people meet the first and third Sundays of the month to play RummiKub. Larry and I realized after we had played a couple of games that Mom's set was missing a tile, a blue three. A friend lent me her unused set, but it doesn't have the same meaning as playing with the same tiles that my mother used for so many years. (If anyone has an incomplete RummiKub game with a blue three still in the bag, send it my way please! My mom and I will thank you!)

Just like my mother and my mother-in-law, I love meeting regularly with friends and family to share a game, food, and conversation. Games not only bring people together but also bring back memories of time spent with those you love and with whom you share a history. As they say in New Jersey, I *oije* everyone to give games a try.

The Jewish World, June 22, 2017

Life Lessons From My Mom

Frances 'Fradyl' Cohen was one special lady, and I was blessed to have her as my mother. She taught me many things during her long life, lessons that I hopefully will pay forward to my children and grandchildren.

Lesson One: There is always room at the table for more.

Six Cohens crowded around the kitchen table in Keeseville, but there was always room for more. Our school friends were always welcome. Salesmen coming through Keeseville on their Upstate New York route often joined us with a half an hour's notice. We had large Sunday lunches with our relatives from Chateauguay and Brushton, and they often stayed late enough to catch a second meal before driving the hour or so back home. Much of our family lived in New York City, and their visits never lasted less than a week.

When the number of people surpassed room in the kitchen, we always could pull out the oak table that held about twenty people in the dining room. And the pot was always full. The Grand Union was less than a two-minute walk from our house, and we frequently did last-minute runs before it closed at 5:30. Besides, Mom always cooked for a family twice our size, and she always had ways to stretch the food so everyone came away satisfied.

Lesson Two: Set an example for your children.

We rarely heard my mother swear. Once in a while, she would spit out a "damn," but that was the extent of our mother's four-letter-word vocabulary. Except for one time when my sister was in college.

In December 1960, Laura came home for winter break from her freshman year at Geneseo State. She had learned a great deal in those first three months, and one lesson was how to curse. She colored her conversations with words that had never been heard in that old house in Keeseville. My mother listened but didn't reprimand Laura. Instead, she peppered her own conversations with profanities. Laura, shocked, said to

Mom, "You never curse! What happened?"

"We sent you off to college so you can get a good education," Mom replied. "We're spending a lot of money for that education. So if my college-educated daughter can swear like a drunken sailor, so can I."

Laura never swore in front of Mom again.

Lesson Three: You are never too old to pursue your dreams.

My mother was the family story teller. Give her an opening, and she would regal any audience with stories of her grandparents' and parents' lives in Russia, of her early years of marriage to "My Bill," of their life in small towns and smaller apartments in the North Country, and of raising four children. Soon after moving from Florida to an independent living facility near us, my mother joined a writing group. Initially she was concerned that her stories, which she had always been shared aloud, would come across as unpolished and boring in written form. She was delighted when her fellow authors told her that she had a natural flair for story-telling. By the time she passed away in 2011, she had written over one hundred typed pages of family history.

Just like Grandma Moses, my mother found she had an undiscovered talent late in life. She always used it as a life lesson for us. "You are never too old to pursue your dreams," she told us. "Look at me! I became a writer in my eighties!" Recently, I have explored ways to self-publish my mother's stories in book form. No, there are no sex scenes or profanity. But it is a good read.

Lesson Four: Changing with the times is sometimes a good thing!

I was a member of the Hadassah Book Group, and on occasion my mother would join me at the meetings. One month, the selection was *This is How I Leave You,* Jonathan Tropper's hilarious account of a dysfunctional Jewish family's week of sitting Shiva. At synagogue one evening, I mentioned to a friend that my mother would be attending the meeting.

"Your mother is reading that book?" she exclaimed. "Why, it's filled with sex scenes and obscenities. I am surprised you even told her about the novel."

"My mom is fine with it," I said. "She's pretty cool!"

At that moment, my mother joined us. "Barbara is surprised you are reading Tropper's book," I explained. "She thinks it's too racy for you."

"I'm loving it," said my mom. "In fact, I now know why no one has published *my* stories. They are not racy enough. I am going to start adding colorful language and sex scenes. THEN maybe I could finally get in print!" Okay, so my sister couldn't swear back in 1960, but my mom could consider it fifty years later if it would advance her writing career!

Recently, my daughter Julie shared a memory of my buying her a gold dress for a middle school dance "I must have tried on ten or twenty dresses before we bought that one," Julie said. Even when she decided not to go to the dance, Julie tried the outfit on another ten or twenty times before she had me return it. "You always had patience for me for stuff like that" she concluded. "Thank you."

I didn't remember the story, but I was so grateful that Julie shared it with me. I wonder if Mom would remember any of the stories I shared above. But I know she would be grateful that *I* remember and that I love and miss her every day.

Summertime and the Swimming Is Easy

As schools let out for the summer, children head to the beach or the pool. Fortunately, my own first experiences with swimming certainly did not seriously hurt my current enjoyment of the sport.

In 1952, my parents moved our family from Potsdam to Keeseville. Both were small upstate New York towns. But whereas Potsdam had a college, including the Crane School of Music, Keeseville was a fairly poor mill town. Soon after my father took over as manager of Pearl's Department Store, the business at Prescott's Lumber, the company that made wooden television cabinets, slowed as manufacturers moved to less expensive metal cases.

Our new home, however, had one major advantage. Keeseville was located less than four miles from Port Douglass, a lovely spot on Lake Champlain that offered a sandy beach with a diving raft a hundred yards off shore. My mother grew up within walking distance of Coney Island's beach and boardwalk and loved the water. She was determined to get her license so she could drive us to the beach herself during our summer vacations.

As we lived only a block away from Pearls, my mother would walk me to the store, hand me over to my father, and then drive away with Mr. Holdridge for her weekly driving lesson. While Dad managed the cash register, I sat in a back corner of the old building, listening to 78 RPM records: Walt Disney's *Snow White and the Seven Dwarfs;* Brothers Grimm and Hans Christian Anderson stories read by Danny Kaye; James Thurber's *The Thirteen Clocks*. Mom passed her driver's test on her third try. Soon after, she got her license in the mail, and I got to take those special records home to listen again and again on our family photograph.

Every summer afternoon, weather permitting, Mom would pile all of us into the station wagon, along with whatever friends tagged along.

We would happily bounce our seat-beltless way to beach, nestled between towels, a couple of chairs, a cooler filled with snacks and drinks, and—once Bobbie was born—a playpen and a diaper bag. Once we got there, we dumped everything onto the sand. Mom would sit in a chair chatting with her friends as we ran into the usually freezing water. (Remember that this was Upstate New York, where the water temperature ranged from sixty degrees in early June to a balmy seventy degrees by August.)

I remember the beach, but I also remember the day—I was probably four—that I waded in too far and found myself over my head. I frantically struggled in three feet of water, going under once, twice, three times. Luckily, a teenager who was standing near my dilemma fished me out and put me back on shore. Sputtering, scared, but safe, I ran back to our blanket.

"I drowneded!" I told my mother. "That's nice, sweetheart," my mother said and went back to her conversation with her friends.

In the years that followed, I, along with many of my friends, took swim lessons at Port Douglass. For six weeks a summer, we caught an 8 a.m. bus provided by the town to take classes taught by high school students. The four years of lessons are etched in my memory through the songs we sang while being shuttled back and forth: *Wake Up Little Susie* (1957); *Tom Dooley* (1958); *Battle of New Orleans (1959);* and *Tell Laura I Love He*r (1960). We'd get home in time for lunch and often a second trip to the beach with Mom behind the wheel.

Around 1961, a swimming pool facility was built near Ausable Chasm. Our family obtained a membership, and we split our time between the sandy beach and the warmer waters of the pool. In 1966, our parents purchased a cottage on Willsboro Bay, across from Burlington, Vermont. We swam off our boat dock and off the small public beach adjacent to our property.

It was also during those summers in Willsboro that I learned how to water ski, resulting in one of the most embarrassing moments of my life: I was sixteen and skiing behind a boat driven by a cute neighbor with his equally cute friend, who was spotting me. All of a sudden I realized that I had lost the top of my two piece bathing suit. I quickly let go of the tow line and submerged myself up to my neck in the middle of the bay. The two "Troy Donahue" look-a-likes brought the boat around to retrieve me. They somehow managed to hold their laughter as they handed me my aqua and white ruffled top—now missing two back buttons—while I handed over my skis.

While in college, I occasionally swam laps in the university's athletic center, but my pool time increased exponentially once Larry and I had children. We joined a neighborhood pool four miles from our house. Adam and Julie played in the water with friends, and I caught a few laps during adult swim. They both took swim lessons and subsequently joined a swim team. We spent many a summer night with timers in our hands as Adam, Julie, and their teammates made their way back and forth the pool with their breaststrokes and freestyles and butterflies.

Larry was not much of a swimmer himself, but he insisted both children get their lifeguard certification. For several years, they got jobs life guarding at our town pools and at college pools. Julie spent two summers managing the pool at The Hole in the Wall Gang Camp in Connecticut, a resort for seriously ill children founded and sponsored by Paul Newman. While Julie occasionally has opportunities to swim, (Nearby mountain-fed Lake Dillon rarely gets above 63 degrees in the summer), Adam still swims regularly in indoor pools near his San Francisco apartment.

In Florida, I swim in our neighborhood pool several times a week. The water is heated to 82 degrees, so warm for my Upstate blood that I have been known to do laps when the air temperature is under sixty degrees. I am a strong swimmer, gliding slowly but steadily back and forth in my lane for forty, fifty minutes without a break. But once in a great while, I inhale a mouthful of water, start choking, and lean on the side of the pool to catch my breath. For that short moment I remember once upon a time, I "drowneded," but I have lived to tell the tale.

The Jewish World, May 11, 2017

Guess Who's Coming to Dinner

He drew a circle that shut me out—
Heretic, a rebel, a thing to flout.
But Love and I had the wit to win:
We drew a circle that took him in!
      Edwin Markham

According to the Bipartisanship Policy Center, our country's history of working across the aisle can be traced back to as early as 1787. Our founding fathers, struggling with congressional representation regarding the populations of the colonies, reached what later was known as the Great Compromise. It was decided that our new government would exist with a proportional House of Representatives and a Senate with equal representation. Once adopted, both sides felt vindicated.

At their best, and despite their differences, presidents and parties have worked together to use compromise for the common good of our country. Lincoln created his "team of rivals" because he believed that he had no right to deprive the country of its strongest minds simply because they sometimes disagreed with him. In the last sixty years, the Civil Rights Act (1964); putting man on the moon (1977); the Endangered Species Act (1973); the American's with Disabilities Act (1990); welfare reform (1996), and No Child Left Behind (2001) all were put into effect because of compromise.

In the current political climate, compromise appears to be all but impossible. Lines have been drawn in the sand, pitting the Republican majority against the Democratic minority with unprecedented rancor. Nuclear options, closed door sessions, and a proliferation of what is regarded as "fake," exaggerated, and even inflammatory news have torn our country apart in ways that many of us—from gifted historians to concerned citizen—cannot remember.

The battle has spilled over to our personal lives, dividing family and friends. The situation has become so flammable that recommendations on how to get along with family and friends with differing political views have become hot topics on everything from television to newspaper articles to Miss Manners. How do we deal with its aftermath when where one stands—whether to the left, to the right, or in the middle—when politics become personal?

I myself had become caught up in the "us versus them" mentality. In the months before the election, I had spent hours watching television, listening to podcasts, and reading articles—usually with left leaning perspectives. Sharing all this news became a priority, either through social media or animated, face to face conversations.

And it hurt me. I had cut off contact with a relative after a Facebook fight about the election last fall, reconciling only after four months of protracted tension. One of my new neighbors, knowing how devastated I was by the November 8 outcome, had purposely avoided me with little more than a smile and hello. Friends invited me to their get-togethers but suggested I leave my politics at the door. As a result, I decided that I could still do what I need to do—stay informed, call my legislators, volunteer to work during the next election cycle. However, as Miss Manners suggested in her June 25, 2017, column, I was no longer going discuss politics in social situations without mutual consent to do so.

While organizing a small dinner party, I realized how difficult the situation had become. One of the guests, whose leanings were unreservedly to the left, called to see if I was inviting a couple known for their strong Republican views. When I asked him the reason for his request, he told me that he recently had had a heated exchange with the couple regarding politics. He and his wife would feel uncomfortable attending if they were going to be there.

Even though the Republicans were not on the guest list for that evening, his request troubled me. Since the elections, I had heard similar comments from other friends who had questioned my continued friendship with any of "those people" who didn't vote the way they had. I also observed many friends drawing lines in the sand. I came to the realization that enough was enough.

I didn't have a good response for my dinner guests during that phone call, but I do now. When the issue comes up, I tell people, "I will be friends with whom I want. Politics will NOT be a decision in my friendship."

In *Tip and the Gipper: When Politics Worked*, Chris Matthews, the former Chief of Staff for House Speaker Tip O'Neill and MSNBC journalist, reported that the political battles between the House Speaker and President Ronald Reagan were "legendary," but they respected and even liked one another. Reagan often had both Republicans and Democrats—including O'Neill—over for cocktails. "After six," O'Neill would insist, "we are all friends."

The only difference with me, the avowed liberal Democrat, and Tip O'Neill is that I won't limit my friendships to after six o'clock. As Thomas Jefferson so wisely said over two hundred years ago, "I never considered a difference in opinion on politics, in religion, in philosophy, as cause enough in withdrawing from a friend."

So I will continue to have friends for dinner, no matter our political affiliations. We will break bread. We will drink wine. We will laugh and enjoy each other's company. And maybe, just maybe, once in a while, we will "reach across the aisle." We will discuss politics, learn what divides and unites us, and, if necessary, agree to disagree. I only wish the same for our president and the members of our United States Senate and House of Representatives.

The Jewish World, July 6, 2017

From Pizza Boy to Shuksuka Expert

My husband Larry and I missed the Pizza Boy's bris.

Diane Silverman, the future Pizza Boy's mom, and I met in 1977. The two of us, along with several new members, sat together at an event sponsored by Clifton Park Hadassah. Within a year, all the women around the table were expecting. Our son Adam was born in April; the Silverman's daughter Erica came one month later. By the time the eight children were walking, the Hadassah Baby Boom mothers formed a weekly playgroup. One of us baby sat while the seven lucky moms got a break.

"Three years apart" must have been the Hadassah mantra, because six of us delivered our second child in 1981. Diane and Mark's son arrived on March 11. Eight days later, while Todd Harris Silverman was ongoing his rite of passage into Judaism, I was having a planned caesarian section. Obviously, Larry and I couldn't be at their simcha—celebration. Therefore, Diane and Mark announced the birth of our daughter Julie Rose to the large group of mutual friends.

As did our two older children, Julie and Todd grew up together. They were in the same playgroup (Hadassah Baby Boom Two), and the same nursery school class. When I went back to work, Diane watched Julie before school. It was Diane who put Julie, along with Todd, on the bus their first day of kindergarten as I had just started my teaching job.

Julie and Todd were close—maybe too close! At the end of first grade, their teacher recommended the two friends be in separate classes as "Julie was leading Todd around by the nose."

Todd was a frequent guest at our house, and he loved his pizza. Larry nicknamed him "Pizza Boy," a moniker that stuck with him for a long time.

By this time, both of our families had joined Congregation Beth Shalom, and we parents shared responsibilities for the children's religious school carpools. We even were each other's helping families at their bar/bat mitzvahs.

Early in his religious education, Todd felt the strength and pull of his Jewish roots. Growing up in a kosher home, Todd lived in a family that actively participated in Judaism through holidays, simchayots, and synagogue membership. Additionally, he felt surrounded by fellow Jews. "You might be hard pressed to find another kid in Upstate New York who felt like the majority of his family's friends were Jewish," Todd said. He realized at a young age that being "a part and parcel of the Jewish community" was important to him.

After his bar mitzvah, Todd joined Schenectady's Temple Gates of Heaven's North American Federation of Temple Youth's (NFTY) chapter. He attended summer camp for three of his four high school years at Kutz Camp, the Reform Movement's youth leadership academy. In 1997 Todd participated in a five-week NFTY-sponsored trip to Israel. He came back bronze-skinned, twenty-five pounds lighter and his eyes opened to Israel.

His religious faith was tested in college. As a theater major at State University of New York at Oswego, Todd found few opportunities for participation in Judaism. Furthermore, the death of three people close to him—an accident, an illness, a suicide—made him seriously question what direction his life would go.

In his last year of college, help came from his NFTY connections. Todd reconnected with a fellow camper from the Kutz Camp, who invited Todd to be on staff at a summer camp in Malibu, California.

Immediately after completing a bachelor's degree in theater, Todd headed to the West Coast. After the summer camp experience, he obtained a job as an elementary school teacher at Brawerman Elementary School in West Los Angeles. His experience at the Jewish day school helped confirm his lifelong belief that he needed to serve the Jewish people. As Todd admitted, his vision was a "romanticized version of spiritual leader, pastoral guide, educator, and keeper of the stories and traditions."

In 2011, Todd enrolled in the Hebrew Union College-Jewish Institute of Religion. As part of his seminary training, he lived for eleven months in Israel, learning the language, the customs, and the politics of the Middle East. He returned to Los Angeles where he spent another five years immersed in history, liturgy, counseling education, pedagogical instruction—everything a series of internships and student pulpits could provide.

Upon his ordination in 2015, Todd learned of a rabbinical position opening in New Orleans, Louisiana. His initial reaction: "There are Jews in New Orleans?" Through the interviewing process, however, Todd learned that the Touro Synagogue, one of the oldest Jewish congregations outside the original thirteen colonies, had a large and active membership. He felt an instant connection to both the shul and the city.

In July 2015, he accepted the position as assistant rabbi and rabbinic director of lifelong learning. Along with life-cycle events and liturgical duties, Todd oversees the synagogue's religious school and Hebrew program and youth group activities.

Todd also continues to teach classes, including courses in Pirkei Avot and rabbinic literature (Midrash, Mishna and Talmud). One of his favorite duties is teaching each semester a four-part cooking class called, "In the Kitchen With Rabbi Silverman." Session topics have included recipes for challah, Jewish soups, Chanukah latkes and sufganiyot, Hebrew for donuts; and shuksuka, a Middle Eastern dish of eggs poached in a cumin-infused sauce of tomatoes, chili peppers, and onions. "I love shuksuka almost as I love pizza," Todd told me.

"I preach and I teach and I learn and I walk to work when it's not 100 degrees with 110% humidity," said Todd. "And I love every second of it."

March 11, 2017, was Rabbi Todd Harris Silverman's thirty-sixth birthday. That evening, he celebrated the holiday of Purim. He helped lead a service, joined his fellow congregants as they twirled their groggers and ate the traditional cookie, hamantashen. Our former Pizza Boy has grown up to become the Pizza Rabbi. I, for one, cannot be prouder of him.

The Jewish World, March 2, 2017

Making the Best Out of Each Day

He was easy to spot. In a room full of frail, elderly people, Marc and his motorized wheelchair loomed large. His six-foot four-inch thin frame rested on the chair, his head on the headrest, and his face inches away from the straw-like device that, through his breathing, powered him around the Daughters of Sarah, a nursing home in Albany, New York.

I had come to Daughters that afternoon to visit Rose, a 99-year old friend. But she had decided to attend a lecture, and I was waiting for her in the community room. So I used my free time to strike up a conversation with the young man, a rarity among the ancient. I learned he had lived at Daughters for eight years, he was thirty-four years old, and he maneuvered his chair around the building chatting with young staff members for companionship—the only people in the facility close to his age. I asked him if I could visit him every week before my time with Rose, and he said, "Sure!"

Maybe because he was just two months older than my son Adam—maybe because he is just a genuinely nice person—no matter—we just clicked. Over the next few weeks, I learned more about his situation. He had become a quadriplegic in a freak motorcycle accident when he was 16—yes, he was wearing a helmet! "Since the accident," Marc told me later, "I really feel I haven't had much choice in anything in life other than give up or carry on."

His parents have been there for him since they got the life-changing phone call that their son had been in a terrible accident. "It was my strong-willed father who especially pushed me to improve my situation," Marc said. "He posted a sign on my computer that read, 'What can I do today to make myself more independent?'"

For the first ten years after his accident, Marc had lived with his parents in their home near Great Sacandaga Lake. Finding good home health care to meet his needs became more problematic, and he and the family decided that Daughters was a better option for him.

Marc never exhibited any bitterness about his situation, and he rarely complained even when he was uncomfortable from his kidney stones or he struggled with breathing. He loved his family and Westerns and fishing and stock car racing. I picked up *101 Things You Should Know About NASCAR* from the library and studied the book so I could talk intelligently with him about the sport. To my husband Larry's amusement, I even started following the results in the newspaper and caught some of the races on the television.

Marc also liked McDonalds, so I often stopped on my way to the nursing home in one the franchise's restaurant a mile from Daughters. The bag of burger and fries left a tantalizing trail of non-kosher—or what Jews know as *treyf*—aromas down the hallway. It took a few times for us to find a rhythm as I fed him: two bites of the Big Mac, two fries, and two sips of soda. Repeat. He loved chocolate, so I usually brought him brownies or chocolate chip cookies, which he saved for later.

Marc owned a fully equipped handicap accessible van, which was kept in the nursing home parking lot. It took me a while to get the courage to take him for outings. One beautiful fall day, however, I asked Marc if he wanted to go for a ride. "Sure!" he said with a huge smile. He guided me through the process of opening up the back door, pushing him up the ramp, pulling his chair back to compensate for his height, and locking the mechanism in place. I slid behind the steering wheel and began our adventure.

We drove up the Northway and across the Twin Bridges. We got an ice cream cone at the Country Drive-In and then sat in a small park near the Mohawk River. The autumn foliage was at its peak, and the sky was a brilliant blue. We had a little scare when the battery light on his van went on. But I managed to deliver him and his vehicle safely back to Daughters.

Over the next three years, I visited Marc on a regular basis, even after Rose passed away. Weather permitting, we would take a field trip—a Chinese restaurant, Five Guys, Walmart, a local mall. Our excursions taught me much about what Marc endures. Adults watched us furtively as I fed him wonton soup; children gawked and asked their parents loud questions as the two of us browsed an aisle in the Christmas Tree Shop. When we stopped in a hair salon, the beautician directed her questions to me until I said emphatically, "Marc is perfectly capable of telling you how he wants his hair cut."

There were many weeks I could not visit Marc—Larry and I were traveling, either Marc or I was sick, or bad weather prevented me from driving the sixteen miles down the Northway. But no matter, I treasured each of those visits with him.

When Larry and I decided to relocate to Florida, telling Marc about our impending move was one of the hardest conversations I had during our transition. Visits from family and other friends were—to me—too few and far between, and Daughters' staff could not drive Marc in his van due to liability issues.

As Larry and I packed up our house, we needed to find a home for four photo collages that we had created from our trips. We brought them to Marc, and he had them hung up on the wall next to his family pictures and a digital photo album we had gotten him the previous Christmas.

On the last visit before we left, Marc and I decided to keep in touch through e-mails. I also promised him that I would mail him a postcard every Monday. On my last visit, I gave him a hug and cried as I made my way across the parking lot past his big blue van to my car.

When Larry and I came back the Albany for Thanksgiving five months later, our second stop with our rental car was Daughters. The first was a stop at Panera Bread for a brownie to bring to Marc. "We were in the neighborhood and thought you could use some chocolate," I said, as we surprised him in his room. On the wall were the photo collages and all the postcards that I had sent him from Florida and Colorado and California.

Marc continues to reside in Daughters of Sarah. He has had a couple of surgeries and several serious health scares. His postcard collection grows, some I purchased during our travels and some given to me by friends and members of the Solivita Travel Club.

In February, Marc celebrated his thirty-ninth birthday. He continues to carry on, to remain positive.

"I have some bad days when I am in pain or can't breathe," Marc told me. "But every day I get up and put a smile on my face. I try to make the best out of each day because I believe that someone always has it worse than I do."

And every day, I am grateful that Marc is my friend.

The Jewish World, November 24, 2017

FLI's

I have spent half my life looking for things I've misplaced. I have spent the other half finding things for my husband Larry that he claims I have lost to make his life more difficult.

Recently I was visiting my daughter Julie, her husband Sam, and my granddaughter Sylvie in Colorado. That morning, I had unplugged my charging cord for my phone from the power strip next to my bed. I was sure that I had plugged it into a kitchen outlet. Later in the morning, however, the only charger, looking mysteriously larger than mine, was connected to Julie and Sam's iPad.

"Sam, are you using my plug to charge your iPad?" I asked.

"No," said Sam. "That one is mine."

I spent a good chunk of the next few hours looking for my missing cord. I looked in my traveling charger case, my pocket book, my suitcase. I rechecked the outlet next to my bed and every other outlet in the house. After we returned from a walk and lunch on Main Street, I rechecked the outlet, my charger bag, the pocketbook, the suitcase. Then I pulled off all the bedding "Maybe it got tangled in the sheets when I was making the bed?" I thought. Missing in action. Julie just rolled her eyes. Mom has lost something—AGAIN.

Misplacing something is part of my personality. Keys. Cell phone. My favorite water bottle. Sun glasses. Larry has grudgingly accepted that every time we head out, we have to allow enough time for me to make one last frantic trip into the house to search for my frequently lost or left behind items (which I refer to as FLIs)

I know that my misplacing things is not tied to cognitive impairment, a concern as I work my way through my sixties. I have not yet found my cell phone in the freezer or my keys in the microwave. Thankfully, my losses are usually a result of multitasking or not giving myself enough time to put the item in its proper spot in the first place. To compensate, I have established assigned places for the FLIs. My keys go in a pewter bowl near the door to the garage. The cell phone goes on the kitchen counter, plugged into the permanent charger. My favorite water bottle gets rinsed and put back into the refrigerator. On my good days, the system works.

I've given up on the sunglasses. After several last minute scrambles, I finally purchased several additional pairs for my pocketbook, each car, the beach bag, the lanai. This system also works—on my good days.

Larry, on the other hand, rarely loses anything. His keys, his wallet, the checkbook, even his clothes, are organized in such a way that he can find them quickly and without angst. He even has a system for items on his desk, where he can locate exactly what he needs from the piles that totally defy my sense of order.

Unfortunately, as we share the same house, our lives—and stuff—intersect. For example, we share laundry duty, but it is usually on my watch that one of his socks goes missing.

"What did you do with my Smart Wool?" he demands.

"You're missing one?" I respond. And the search begins. The washing machine. The dryer. Then the rest of the laundry to see if it got stuck to a recalcitrant t-shirt or pair of shorts. The loss is usually NOT permanent.

The second most FLI is the checkbook. Larry has a particular Spot for it. There are times, however, that I need it. Invariably, I either don't put it back in the Spot fast enough or I don't put it exactly where it belongs. Then, the scenario begins.

"MAR-i-lyn! Where is the checkbook?" The situation is quickly resolved—EXCEPT when we moved into our Florida house. One of us put the checkbook in a "safe place" before we left for a long trip to Colorado. If anyone has any suggestions as to where our "safe" place was, please contact me. Two and a half years later, the checks are still missing.

Remember I said that Larry *rarely* loses anything? Let me relate the Famous Missing Fleece Incident.

While we were still living in Upstate New York, our son Adam came home in July for a visit. One surprisingly cool morning, the three of us went on a bike ride. Larry had Adam use his road bike, and he took his hybrid.

A couple of weeks after Adam left, Larry asked me what I had done with the University of Rochester fleece he had worn on the bike ride.

"I have no idea," I said. "I probably washed it and put it in your closet."

"Well, it's missing," Larry said.

Thus began a three-month intermittent search. I checked every closet and dresser in the house. I called Adam and asked if he had taken it back with him to California. *Nada.*

"Maybe you gave it to the Salvation Army," Larry said. "I can't believe you would give away my favorite fleece to the Salvation Army."

On a cool, overcast day at the end of October, Larry and I decided to go on a bike ride. The roads were wet from a recent rain, so we took our hybrid bikes for better traction. Halfway through the ride, it began to rain again. Larry paused to put his phone, which was in a case on the handlebar, into the saddle bag to better protect it.

"Hey! Look what I found!" Larry exclaimed. "It's my missing fleece! I must have put it in there in July when it began to warm up on our bike ride with Adam."

"YOU misplaced it!" I said. "Don't you feel bad for accusing ME of losing it?"

"No, that's okay," said Larry. "All's well that ends well."

And the charging cord I "lost" in Colorado? Turns out that Sam had rolled it up and put it into a canister where he and Julie stash all their extra cords. So I actually wasn't at fault that time either.

Elizabeth Bishop wrote: "The art of losing isn't hard to master; /so many things seem filled with the intent /to be lost that their loss is no disaster." In my world, losing "stuff" may be a problem. As long as I keep what is important—my family, my friends, my memories—it will just be *small* stuff.

The Jewish World, May 11, 2017

Loveys

Rerun, like his distant English relative Paddington Bear, has had quite an interesting life.

Two days after my daughter Julie was born, "Big Brother" Adam visited her in the hospital with a brown stuffed bear in tow. He and my husband Larry had picked it out at the toy store that morning. They named him "Rerun," the moniker—hats off to Charles Schultz—we had given my increasingly growing tummy during the pregnancy. Rerun took his place at the corner of the hospital bassinet, allowing Adam to recognize his sister in the nursery. Julie reciprocated the day she came home from the hospital when Adam found a Spiderman doll waiting on his pillow.

Thus began Rerun's journey through Julie's life. He was a permanent resident of her crib, her "big girl" bed, and her college dorm room. Rerun traveled cross country with Julie when she started her new life in Colorado. He even had a place on Julie's bed stand after she married Sam.

And now my daughter's daughter has her own lovey. Sylvie latched onto Foxy when Julie brought the big-eyed Beanie Boo home from an airport gift shop. Sylvie carries him with her everywhere, tucked securely under her arm. When he isn't being held, Foxy watches over Sylvie when she eats and when she takes her bath. And every night, Foxy accompanies Sylvie to bed, where they are joined by Rerun, who now has a special spot in the crib.

While writing this story, I posted a request on Facebook for people to share their "lovey" story about a toy or item with which they or someone they knew were totally attached. Over a dozen people responded—with tales as far away as Israel. Anne Rothenberg shared that her grandson Amiad is attached to large stuffed dog named "Clavlavi" ("puppy" in Hebrew). The dog has been a part of their family for almost a decade. "He is pretty bald from years of stroking and washing," Anne said, "but the whole family loves him so much that he is included in all family pictures."

People reached back decades into their own childhood to talk lovingly of their favorite toy or blanket. Lee Ryan, a former student, wrote, "At age sixty, I still have Teddy. Of course, I can be without him, but I am grateful he's still around."

Susan Lenigan recalled that over sixty years ago, her sister Judy had her "Kitty." As time went by, the stuffed animal's eyes fell out and his face became faded. During one of her visits, their grandmother decided to "fix" Kitty while Judy was in school. She sewed on new button eyes and painted on a new face. When Judy came home and saw Kitty, she cried and ran away from her precious companion. She gradually—and grudgingly—accepted the imposter.

Linda LaFlure Nelson also learned that loveys often were best untouched. She and her daughter still remember the sad day that Linda washed Sara's beloved "Blanky" "Sara burst into tears, sobbing that it no longer smelled like her." Linda said. "I felt like a bad mommy." Blanky ended up as nothing more than a smelly knotted ball of tattered material. Nevertheless, Sara, now in her thirties, has Blanky tucked away in a drawer in her home.

And like Rerun, loveys have traveled the country—and world. Becky Silverstein's daughter Evey had a crocheted pink blanket with yellow edging that Becky received at her baby shower. Evey held it all day, flipping the corners back and forth repeatedly, self-soothing and settling herself down. Whenever Evey was hurt or fussy, Becky would sing "Mr. Blankey makes it better, yes, he does." It went everywhere: in the car, in the crib, in the high chair, in the playpen, on every family vacation. Eventually, Mr. Blankey also went with sixteen-year-old Evey for a two-week stay in Scotland and for a three-month trip to Israel after she graduated from the Jewish Day School in Maryland. Mr. Blankey then went to college in Boston, moved with her and her fiancee to California, and went on their honeymoon cruise in the Mediterranean. Now Mr. Blankey has a place of honor on their bed in San Jose, California, providing a cozy napping spot for their dog, Kiwi. As Becky said, "Mr. Blankey still makes it all better."

Losing loveys can become a major emergency. Sharon McLelland's daughter's cow, which still is "alive" with more stitches than body, once was FedEx'd overnight soaking wet as he was so needed. And those emergencies sometimes spill over to adulthood. Lynn Urgenson's daughter Sue had a hand crocheted "Blan-key" that she slept with even up into her adult years. When Susie moved to Israel, Lynn forwarded it to her. Unfortunately, it got lost in the mail. When the package finally was returned to Lynn six months later with "Address Unknown" stamped on it, Lynn decided to avoid further heartache and deliver the tattered blanket in person next time she saw Sue. "My granddaughter Sarit has a beautiful one I made for her," said Lynn, "but she doesn't have same attachment!"

Can one avoid disaster with back-ups? My daughter has two *identical* Foxy's tucked away in case Sylvie loses her constant companion. Sometimes, however, even that plan backfires. Judy Lynch's daughter Katie slept with a stuffed panda. When Katie was twenty months old, Judy went back to work and bought a second Pandy so one bear could stay at home and the second could stay at the sitter's. Katie became attached to both Pandys and had to have both of them in both places. Judy recalled," Who knows how many times we had to drive back to the sitter's when we realized we'd left a Pandy behind!"

Fortunately, some children accept change. Jackie Betters' grandson had a blanket named "Meme" that he slept with every night. His mom washed it so much from his dragging it everywhere with him that it got pathetically thin. She folded it in half and sewed it. After several more washings, it got thinner. So she folded it again into a twelve inch square and, eventually into a six inch square. His mom has it tucked away in her dresser just in case he should ever need it again—even though he is now a grown man with a newborn son of his own.

Now that children and parents are gearing up for school opening, don't be surprised to find loveys hidden away to provide needed security. Over thirty years ago, Julie Thompson Berman's son had a beloved "blankie." All through kindergarten he carried a tiny piece of it in his pocket. He never took it out, but he would just put his hand in his pocket, touch it, and be comforted.

Rerun. Foxy. Teddy. Clavlavi. Kitty. Pandy. Assorted pieces of tattered, smelly blankets. Each one treasured, loved, and often still part of their owners' lives.

The Jewish World, August 3, 2017

Her Own Best Advocate

During our recent stay in Colorado, my husband Larry and I hiked to Adam's Falls in Rocky Mountain National Park. As we were finishing our walk, we saw a group of young adults with intellectual disabilities hiking up the trail. We learned later that they were on a field trip with Adam's Camp, part of a non-profit organization which offers intensive therapy, family support, and recreation in a camp environment for children and youth with special needs.

Seeing the group brought me much joy. On that beautiful afternoon in Colorado, the campers were happy, glowing, involved. Less than fifty years ago, they would have had a good chance of being marginalized at best, institutionalized at worst. Claudia "Clyde" Lewis' sister Andrea Gregg almost suffered that fate.

Clyde's parents met in high school, and Clyde was born soon after graduation. Her father, Robert Pinard, went into the Navy and would not meet her until she was nineteen years old.

Her mother Iola married Arthur Gregg when Clyde was ten years old. Andrea was born two years later. Clyde, her mother, and step-father were delighted with the newest member of their New Hampshire family.

When Andrea was about six months old, the pediatrician recommended that Iola take Andrea to the Dartmouth Medical Center, citing respiratory problems as the reason for an evaluation. "My mother recalled Andrea getting a great deal of attention," said Clyde. "She thought it was because there was only one other baby on the medical center's floor."

Then the doctors gave Iola the life-changing news. "You realize that your little girl has Down syndrome, don't you?" Predicting that Andrea would never walk, talk, or function normally, the doctors recommended placing Andrea in an institution and "forgetting about her."

The devastated parents reached out to the family for help. Iola's brother insisted that the family move near them in California, one of the few states at the time that offered special programs for children with intellectual disabilities. Iola and Arthur decided to make the move as soon as Clyde finished her school year in June.

Clyde's parents didn't share the news of Andrea's condition with her until the family was already on their way to California. "It was the saddest car trip of my life," said Clyde. "I cried the entire time, not able to accept that my beautiful little sister was different."

Once the four settled in Santa Ana, however, Clyde didn't let Andrea's differences get in the way of loving her. She took her sister under her wing, mothering her and helping her learn to walk and talk. It changed Clyde's outlook on life. "If you wanted to be my friend," recalled Clyde," you had to accept the fact that Andrea would be tagging along. She was my sidekick."

Clyde also advocated for her sister when Andrea started special education classes. "Andrea was always bugging me when I was doing my homework," said Clyde. "So I put up a chalkboard and started her on her ABCs. Soon she was writing her own name and reading. I went to her teachers and showed them what she could do." Andrea also learned to write in cursive, which she regarded as one of her greatest accomplishments. "She loved telling people she could sign her 'John Hancock,'" said Clyde.

Clyde graduated Santa Ana Valley High School in 1963 (an unknown band, The Beach Boys, played at her senior prom) and enrolled in UC Fullerton. In her junior year, her birth father, Robert Pinard connected with Clyde and asked her to come to Vermont that summer to meet him, his wife, and her seven half-sisters and brothers. Clyde agreed to go as long as she could also bring Andrea.

Robert owned and operated the ski shop/shoe store at Norwich University, a private military college. He asked Hal Lewis, one of the cadres breaking in the incoming cadets to "watch out" for the daughter whom he had never met. "I fell in love with Clyde AND Andrea," said Hal. After her college graduation, Clyde flew back to the East Coast to attend Hal's graduation. The two were married and settled in New Hampshire.

After she graduated from her special education program, Andrea worked different jobs at Wendy's, McDonald's, and a local supermarket. When Arthur retired, he, Iola and Andrea moved to Charlestown, New

Hampshire, to be closer to Clyde, Hal, and their support. Clyde would drive the six-hour round trip from her home in Plainstov at least once a week to take them to stores and to doctors' appointments.

Andrea enrolled in a sheltered workshop program. She also became involved in a local Special Olympics track and field program. Although she wasn't good at the sport, her reading and writing skills made her an ideal "administrator" for the team. Her success in those duties resulted in her appointment to the board of the New Hampshire's Governor's Council for the Disabled. Once a month, she went to Concord to participate in the meeting and attend workshops on how to handle themselves and their interactions with others.

Both parents passed away by the time Andrea was forty-eight years old, and she came to live with Clyde and Hal. They set her up in the lower level of their home, in an area with her own private entrance that contained a bedroom, a living room, and a kitchenette. Andrea was thrilled. "I never had my own apartment before!" she exclaimed.

Soon after her suitcases were unpacked, Andrea and Clyde made a trip to Walmart to buy needed items for her new "apartment." After trip through all the aisles, they headed to the check-out line with a shopping cart filled with kitchen items, towels, and bedding. Suddenly, two women pushed in front of Andrea with their cart.

"Move your fat ass," one of the women told Andrea.

"What did you say to me?" Andrea said.

"You heard her," the second woman said. "She said, 'Move your fat ass!'"

Andrea pulled herself up to her full five-foot height. "People see my disability when they look at me," Andrea said loudly. "People can see *your* disability when you open your mouth!"

As the two women deserted their cart and slunk away, the people waiting in line burst into applause and cheers.

Clyde beamed with pride. "I guess you can take care of yourself," she said.

"I guess those advocacy classes are finally paying off!" said Andrea.

Andrea lived with Clyde and Hal until her death at 53 from heart disease, a complication of her Down syndrome. Clyde keeps a picture on her refrigerator of her beloved sister. They are standing together, with their arms around each other, smiling broadly. "She will always be with me in my heart," said Clyde.

Scott Hamilton, the Olympic skater said, "The only disability in life is a bad attitude." Thanks to advances in public education, the intellectually challenged have opportunities to reach their full potential. Thanks to programs like Adam's Camp and Special Olympics, these same individuals have opportunities for recreation and personal fulfillment. And thanks to people like Andrea, Clyde, and her family, we all are made aware that every individual—no matter what their challenges—can offer much to our world.

The Jewish World, August 17, 2017

Loving the Body I Have

Virginia went to her grave hating her body.

A lifetime member of Weight Watchers, I had been attending meetings in Clifton Park since 2013. I had reached a goal weight approved by my doctor, but I continued to find the weekly meetings helpful in keeping myself honest as well as connecting with fellow "warriors"—mostly women—who were fighting their battle against the scale.

When I moved to Florida in June 2015, I immediately joined a local Weight Watchers group, where I met Virginia, another "regular" who I guessed was in her late seventies. With the help of her walker, she was always willing to pull herself up and share her experiences on her weight loss journey. By the end of 2016, she had reached her one-hundred-pound loss milestone, and her self-confidence grew. Over the last year, however, she plateaued and then saw the scale inch back up. Hoping to lose at least fifty additional pounds, Virginia tried hard to reverse her negativity. "Every day, I say to myself in the mirror, 'Virginia, you are going to reach your goal!'" But she continued to struggle with her weight and self-image.

On August 24, Virginia was noticeably absent. "I have sad news," said the leader at the start of the meeting. "Virginia passed away this past week of cancer."

I was saddened, angry, and afraid. Saddened that we didn't know she was dying of cancer; angry that she went to her grave hating herself for being overweight, hating the person in the mirror for that number on the scale; afraid that I too would be obsessed with the scale, not comfortable with my body, until my dying day.

As a young child, I was so small —sixteen pounds at two years old—my nickname was Peanut. But my family's diet, heavy on brisket and bread and baked good and bowls and bowls of ice cream, along with genetics, finally won out. By eight years old, I was chubby.

When I hit puberty, I lost weight and gained height. The good news was that I inherited my father's long thin legs and striking blue eyes. The not-so-good-news, at least in my "striking blue eyes," was that I also inherited my paternal aunts' broad shoulders, short waists, and tendency to pile on the pounds. While never medically obese (20% over one's ideal weight) my entire adult life, I found myself at times overweight. I joined Weight Watchers for the first time when I was twenty-six, beginning a lifetime of cycling in and out of weight loss programs.

Wherever I am on the scale, I have always been thankful for a healthy, strong body. My health indicators—blood pressure, cholesterol, blood sugar— are all in the normal range. I bike, hike, walk, take exercise classes. But, like Virginia, I still have found myself unhappy with my weight and my body image.

I am not alone. A 2012 study of women fifty and older published in International *Journal of Eating Disorders* found that 71% were currently trying to lose weight; 79% felt that weight or shape played a "moderate" to "the most important" role in their self-concept; 70% were dissatisfied with their weight and shape compared to when they were younger; and 84% were specifically dissatisfied with their stomachs. In a similar study published in 2013 in the *Journal of Women and Aging*, it was found that the majority of women aged 50 and older are not satisfied with the way they look, with only 12% of participants sampled reporting body image satisfaction.

The causes of obsession with the scale and our perceived negative self-image are as close as the television in our living rooms, the magazines on our coffee table, the movies playing at our local theater, the advertisements bombarding us daily. In a 2013 article on women's body image in *Slate*, Jessica Grose notes that media images of ridiculously thin women surround us. "We live in a culture where thinness and beauty are highly valued for women, and wealth and success are often considered to go hand in hand with a slim figure." She cites the resulting negative effects: a preoccupation with diet, low self-esteem, low self-confidence and/or never feeling that one's body is adequate.

The damage that such images creates starts in girls as young as nine and ten (over fifty percent feel better about themselves if they are on a diet), continues into middle age and, as in the case of Virginia, persists into old age. In her article "Body Image: How It Affects Middle-Aged Women," Crystal Karges captures the continuum. "The little girl who once felt ashamed of her body or unsure of her place in the world may find that she is still unable to accept or love herself in the later years of her life."

Maybe society is changing. The Fat Acceptance movement seeks to change anti-fat bias in social attitudes. Companies including JC Penney, Nike, and Unilever have launched campaigns meant to change how gender is portrayed in their advertising. Even Mattel, which has faced criticism that its female dolls promoted unhealthy body ideals, underwent a revolution. The 2016 line of Barbies introduced three new body types in addition to the stick-thin original—tall, petite, and curvy (or what I like to call *zaftig*—Yiddish for pleasantly plump).

My reaction to Virginia's death and my subsequent research has been a learning experience for me. I now recognize that I can honor Virginia's memory by being more accepting and appreciative of my own body—strong, curvy, healthy, imperfect—and of those of others, no matter what their size and shape. I have promised myself to focus less on the number on the scale and more on the benefits I can obtain from maintaining a lifestyle that includes healthy food choices, regular exercise, moderation, and a positive attitude.

In the mold breaking JC Penney ad, one of the "real women" represented states, "You can't love your body for what you hope it turns into without actively loving it for what it is today." Virginia and all of us women who battle the scale and, more importantly, our self-image, need to love ourselves where we are right now.

The Jewish World, October 12, 2017

Moving Mountains: Creating a Legacy

"I will grieve for a lifetime."
Angela Miller, Founder and facilitator of Bereaved Mamas

After losing her toddler son, Angela Miller mobilized her grief to found and facilitate an on-line grief support, and social group for others who had suffered the death of a child. She recognized that loss parents would move mountains to honor their children and spare others from being unwilling participants in "this crappy club called child loss."

I know of two such people. Judy and Charlie Lynch's daughter Katie died at the age of 31 after being diagnosed with one of the deadliest forms of blood cancers. To honor their daughter's legacy, the Lynches have moved their own mountains to raise thousands of dollars for cancer research.

Until Katie's devastating illness, the Lynchs, a close-knit loving family, had shared a life filled with many happy memories. Judy, who grew up near Chicago, and Charlie, who grew up in Pennsylvania, had met at Oberlin College and were married soon after graduating. They settled in the Capital Region of New York. Katie was born six years later, on January 16, 1978. Katie was joined by her sister Julia in 1981.

In 1987, our families met through the Knolls Gang, a locally run summer swim team in Clifton Park, New York. Katie and our son Adam were in the same age group, as were Julia and our daughter Julie. The four adults spent the next several years sharing conversation and stopwatch duties at the meets. We became close friends, a friendship that continues today.

Katie stayed chlorinated for many years that followed. She swam for the Colonie Aquatics as well as Shenendehowa swim team. She also joined the high school's cross country ski team. A gifted student, Katie graduated as co-valedictorian of Shenendehowa class of 1996, garnering several academic awards.

Katie attended Drew University in New Jersey on scholarship, where she was named the captain of her swim team. She was inducted into Phi Beta Kappa in 1999 and graduated summa cum laude in 2000. Following graduation, Katie accepted a job as a software developer at Ernst and Young. In 2008, Katie was doing well with her job and was in a serious relationship with a wonderful man she had met two years earlier. Family and friends were looking forward to the announcement giving the joyful news of their engagement.

Instead, that September Judy sent out a heartbreaking e-mail sharing a far different message. "Katie is sick" read the subject line. Katie had been diagnosed with acute myelogenous leukemia (AML).

Even with previously excellent general health and her young age, Katie had at best a 50/50 chance of recovery. An aggressive medical approach was needed— immediately. Katie, always one to accept a challenge, determinedly underwent everything the doctors threw at her—chemotherapy, numerous hospitalizations, painful side effects and biopsies, and countless blood tests and transfusions.

Judy had always relied on running as therapy, a way of coping and "figuring things out." Now her avocation would become her mission— her way to fight for Katie's life. Judy had heard of Team in Training (TNT), the flagship fundraising program for Leukemia and Lymphoma Society. TNT volunteers, many themselves survivors, trained to complete a marathon, half marathon, cycle event, triathlon or hike adventure, while fundraising to support the fight against blood cancers through research, education, and patient services.

Judy signed up with TNT to run in a half marathon in Longbranch, New Jersey. Katie had gone into remission, and Judy regarded the race as a victory lap, with Katie and her now-fiancé meeting Judy at the finish line. Friends and family gladly donated money in Katie's honor to support Judy's efforts. As a result, Judy raised over $12,500.

Tragically, Katie would not watch her mother complete the race. The cancer reoccurred, and she was in the hospital preparing for a stem cell transplant. In the end, Katie's positive attitude, her strong will to live, and undergoing every conceivable treatment were not enough. On October 26, 2009, the Lynches' beautiful, intelligent, courageous daughter succumbed to the disease. She was 31.

Running now became Judy's bridge into life without Katie, a way to move forward and memorialize her daughter. Immediately after the memorial service, Judy signed up for the 2010 Boston Marathon. A torn hamstring delayed that goal until 2011. Meanwhile, she found shorter races—in Atlanta and in the Capital District. Judy made a personal commitment to do one event a year for TNT, raising as much money as she possibly could each time. She has followed these initial efforts with additional races, including two subsequent Boston Marathons and the New Jersey Half Marathon,

With Katie as her inspiration, Judy has also accepted challenges she never would have considered. Judy has expanded her fund-raising efforts to include a triathlon and two one-hundred-mile bike rides. While participating in the event, Judy wears a shirt with Katie's picture interlaid with Runner's Prayer, her message to her daughter. "Run by my side/Live in my heartbeat/Give me strength in my steps./As the cold surrounds, as the wind pushes me/I know you surround me./As the sun warms me, as the rain cleanses me, I know you are touching me, challenging me, loving me./And so I give you this run."

Charlie has been Judy's number one supporter, and he himself supports LLS through his Craft Beers for Cures fundraisers.

"There is no handbook on what to do when the unthinkable happens, no blueprint on how to live your life, how to move forward," wrote Judy in a video she made to honor Katie's legacy. "For us, it is important that something positive result from Katie's death, that we do everything we can to spare other families from the devastation we have experienced."

Since Katie was diagnosed with AML, the Lynches have raised over one hundred and twenty-thousand dollars for blood cancer research. Through their *tzedakah*—their charity and giving—Judy and Charlie have kept Katie's memory alive not only in their hearts but also in the hearts of their many supporters.

The Jewish World, January 29, 2017

Tikkun Olam

A Mensch of a Man

In 2017, for the first time in sixty years, Harry Lowenstein celebrated Rosh Hashanah without his beloved wife Carol. It was a bittersweet occasion, only a few short weeks after what would have been their sixtieth anniversary. But Harry was a survivor as well as a *mensch*, a person with integrity and honor.

Harry Lowenstein was born in Fürstenau, Germany, in 1931, the younger of two children. When he was seven years old, Harry was expelled from school for being a Jew. In 1940, he and twenty members of his family were deported to the Riga ghetto in Latvia. The train carrying approximately one thousand Jews left Bilefeld, Germany on the first night of Chanukah. Someone had brought candles on the crowded compartment and started singing *Ma'oz Tzur,* Rock of Ages. Soon the entire train joined in. That last sweet memory sustained Harry for the next six years.

In the ghetto, his entire family was crowded into a two-room apartment. A year and a half later, the family was sent to the concentration camp of Riga-Kaiserwald, where the men and women were separated. "Return home after this is over to find us," his mother begged before she said goodbye.

One day, Harry found a piece of bread outside a building and brought it to his father to share. "Where did you find this?" his father asked. When Harry told him, his father said, "You just took that bread away from someone who is as hungry as you were. Give it back and apologize." When Harry returned, his father slapped him on the face. "I still can feel that slap," said Harry. "What a lesson in ethics he gave me!"

Soon after, Harry's father fell ill and was sent back to the ghetto, which was liquidated in November 1943. Harry never saw his father again. While in Riga-Kaiserwald, Harry experienced constant fear of being chosen for the gas chamber and the ongoing, intentionally cruel actions by Nazi guards. When Harry stole a piece of bread from a kitchen, Nazi prison guards stood him outside in the freezing cold and blasted a water hose down his shirt. "I thought to myself, ˜I will somehow survive," said Harry. "You learned to live minute to minute—not even hour by hour—to make sure the next day comes."

In the fall of 1944, as the Russian front drew close, the Nazis tried to avoid the Allied forces. Harry, along with thousands of other Jewish prisoners, were shipped by boat to Danzig and then by barge to the Stuthoff concentration camp in Poland. On March 9, 1945, the camp was liberated by the Red Army. He and fellow survivors were brought to a makeshift hospital. For six weeks, he and fellow survivors were fed a diet of oatmeal to help them regain their strength. The next day—and freedom—had come. Remembering his mother's instructions from years earlier, the 14-year-old returned to Fürstenau to reunite with his family. His trip was in vain. He was the sole survivor.

As the High Holy Days approached that fall, Harry visited a fellow survivor, and a group of them went to services in a makeshift synagogue. A Polish Jewish officer serving in the British army asked Harry if he had had his bar mitzvah. When Harry said no, the Polish officer said, "Then you will have your bar mitzvah today, on the first day of Rosh Hashanah, the beginning of the rest of your life."

After spending the next four years in children's homes in Hamburg and Paris, Lowenstein emigrated to the United States in March 1949. He stayed in the Bronx with an aunt and uncle who had emigrated to the United States in 1928. He worked in a butcher shop during the day and attended school at night, trying to build on two years of schooling he had before the war.

In 1952, after serving two years in the army, Harry moved to Florida, where he got a job working in his uncle's clothing shop. "Selling a pair of pants or some shoes was easier than hauling sixty pounds of frozen treyf, [non-kosher food]," said Harry. He hung up his butcher's apron for good.

On February 14, 1957, Harry went on a blind date with Carol Sainker, the daughter of another butcher. After only six weeks of long distance dating (they lived four hours apart), he proposed. They were married on August 18, 1957. Harry and Carol lived in England during

Tikkun Olam

the 1960s, and then moved back to Florida in the 1970's with their three children, Berna, David, and Karen.

In 1974, Harry and Carol took over Goolds, a clothing store in Kissimmee that had previously been run by another uncle, Luther Goold. Carol and he ran the business for thirty years, expanding the building from 1600 to 6000 square feet. As the only department store in town, it sold what everyone wore in Central Florida—jeans, cowboy shirts, and boots. The Lowensteins attended Congregation Shalom Aleichem, which had met since its founding in 1981 at the Kissimmee Women's Club. The Lowensteins began to press for a building of their own. "I saw a synagogue burn," said Harry, "and I was determined to build another one." Starting with a $120,000 contribution from Sandor Salmagne, another Holocaust survivor, the Lowensteins—through their own and friends' contributions—raised another $60,000 for building expenses.

Once Congregation Shalom Aleichem opened, the Lowensteins continued to work tirelessly to obtain a Torah, the prayer books for both every day and holy days, the Torah *rimonim* (finials), and the *yartzheit* (memorial) board, most coming from their own pockets. Carol served as treasurer for over thirty years, and Harry held every position on the board except that of president. "My language skills were not up to my standards," explained Harry.

Rabbi Karen Allen, Congregation Shalom Aleichem's spiritual leader, expressed her admiration for the extraordinary and exemplary hospitality that characterized the Lowensteins at home as well as in their role as congregation leaders. "It was my privilege to be their guest on many Friday nights after services, and I will always be grateful for the kindness and generosity of their elegant graciousness," said Rabbi Allen. "It is easy to understand how such caring and sensitive people could have created a successful business that for so many years contributed greatly to the growth of our community."

Their daughter Karen remembered her parents as "the most loving couple" with an old-school work ethic that they instilled in their children: "Be honest, put in 110%, be truthful, and remember that being on time was being late." Karen has especially fond memories of the High Holy Days. "My mom would spend weeks cooking. On the night of the dinner, the table was set with our finest china, silverware, and crystal, with flowers gracing the center."

Unfortunately, Carol faced major health problems throughout most her life. She experienced a heart attack at thirty-eight years old, which began years of cardiac issues. "Each time she was hospitalized," recalled Karen, "we thought it was the end. We were blessed to have her for so long." Carol died peacefully on February 10, 2017, at the age of eighty-one.

Despite his grief, Harry remains intensely committed to the Congregation Shalom Aleichem, its building and its spiritual aspects. He quietly continues his *tzedakah*—his charity—to many others.

As he has done for many years, he gives frequent talks about his Holocaust experiences to local synagogues, schools, and other public venues. Video accounts of his first-person narrative are on file in both The Holocaust Memorial Resource and Education Center of Florida in Orlando and Stephen Spielberg's University of Southern California Survivors of the Shoah Visual History Foundation.

Harry shows no bitterness about his experiences in World War II. "The Nazis couldn't take away from me who I am in my heart," said Harry. "They could not change me. I was and still am a Jew."

And most importantly, Harry is a *mensch*—a person of integrity and honor. I know many people who share this sentiment: May you live for many more High Holy days in which you make your life and Carol's memory a blessing.

The Jewish World, September 22, 2017

A Soldier, An Orphan, and a Photographer

A body of an American solider lying peacefully in the snow in a battlefield in Belgium. A Jewish boy in Brooklyn orphaned twice by World War II. And the world-renowned photographer who connected the two. This is their story.

Samuel Tannenbaum was born on July 10, 1942, in Washington DC to Henry and Bertha Fiedel Tannenbaum. Less than two years later, Henry was drafted into the United States Army. Bertha and Sam moved to Williamsburg section of Brooklyn to be closer to their families. After training at Fort Meade, Maryland, Henry was assigned to the 331st Infantry regiment, 883rd division, and was shipped to England. His rifle platoon subsequently fought in battles in France and Luxembourg, which garnered Henry several medals.

Between December 16, 1944, and January 25, 1945, on the border of Belgium and Luxembourg, Allied and German troops were engaged in what would later be known as The Battle of the Bulge, one of World War II's deadliest fights. On January 11, Tannenbaum and his division were ambushed by German soldiers. Only one person—Platoon Sergeant Harry Shoemaker—survived.

When Shoemaker escaped and returned to regimental headquarters, he told the sentry, Corporal Tony Vaccaro, the details of the massacre. Vaccaro and Shoemaker returned to the site the next morning. The two stared at the horrible carnage. If the soldiers had survived, the Germans murdered the wounded and stripped the corpses of their watches and other valuables. Then the Germans rolled their tanks over the dead and dying, crushing them into grotesque, mangled shapes.

Only one figure looked peaceful and untouched by death. The prone body of a lone soldier lay face down, his boots, backpack, helmet and rifle showing through the white snow that blanketed him. Vaccaro pulled out his Argus C vintage camera and captured the scene. Afterward, Vaccaro and Shoemaker cleared away the snow to discover the dead soldier was their army friend, Private Henry Tannenbaum.

Henry Tannenbaum was buried in Henri-Chapelle Cemetery in Belgium with plans to bring his body home. Bertha Tannenbaum, his widow, falsely believed that the transfer would adversely affect her four-year old-son Sam's war orphan benefits. She was against reinternment. Henry's family fought Bertha's decision and won, and Henry's remains were returned to New York in 1946. The disagreement caused the widow's estrangement from the Tannenbaums, isolation from her own family, and her growing mental deterioration. In her mind, Bertha believed that Henry was still alive and working secretly for the FBI. Sam's childhood was filled with his mother's shouting at the ghost of her husband, several psychotic episodes, and even an attempt to kill her son and then commit suicide. "The bullet that killed my father also destroyed my mother's mind and ended my childhood," said Sam.

With "my father dead and my mother crazy," Samuel was forced at a young age to raise himself. He took care of household chores, did the shopping, and, through conniving, even paid the bills. When he was thirteen, he arranged for his own bar mitzvah, fortuitously connecting with his father's family through a Hebrew school classmate. Upon graduating high school, he moved into his own apartment and, supporting himself with a war orphan scholarship and odd jobs, graduated from Brooklyn College.

While Sam was in college, Bertha was evicted from her apartment and was committed to a state mental institution. The eviction resulted in the destruction of the family's belonging, including all artifacts of Sam's family's history. Outside of his name and the date of his death, Sam knew nothing about his father. Sam married, (Bertha didn't come to the wedding; she thought it was another FBI plot), had a daughter Lisa, and divorced. Bertha met and fell in love with Sam's fiancée Rachel, promising her that Henry would return in time for the wedding.

Meanwhile, with the help of the extended family, Sam was putting together pieces of his father's past. Henry was regarded as intelligent with a great sense of humor. He had graduated from the same grade school, high school, and college as his son. Henry worked for the Office of Price Administration and taught Sunday school at a local synagogue. Henry had an inherited bleeding disorder which probably caused the private's quick and peaceful death in Belgium on that bitter cold January day, and that unfortunate disorder was passed on to his son.

In 1986, three years after his mother died, Sam invited his father's family to his daughter Lisa's bat mitzvah. His first cousin, Henry's niece, gave Sam a Victory Mail correspondence that identified Private Henry Tannenbaum's regiment. Sam now had the tool he needed to further research his father's military history.

In 1995, he and his wife Rachel journeyed to Seattle to attend the premiere meeting of the American World War II Orphan Network (AWON). The national organization was composed of the Gold Star children and others classified by the Veterans Administration as war orphans.

At a second AWON meeting in Washington DC in 1996, Sam met several people from Luxembourg who came for the express purpose to meet and thank the children of their liberators. Sam invited several to his home. One of the guests, Renee Schloesser, a journalist, published the Tannenbaum story in a series of articles in a Luxembourg newspaper. Another attendee, Jim Schiltz, was also impressed with Sam's search. When he returned to Luxembourg, Schiltz found a book of photographs of World War Two and specifically, of the 331 Regiment in Luxembourg taken by the sentry Tony Vaccaro.

The picture taken on the battlefield in Ottre was not the only one Tony Vaccaro had captured. Michaelantonio Celestino Onofrio Vaccaro had carried his Argus C with him when he, along with thousands of fellow Allied soldiers, stormed the beaches at Normandy on D-Day. Tony—at first surreptitiously and then with his superiors' approval—went on to take thousands of pictures of Allied campaigns in Normandy and Germany.

After the war, Tony stayed in Europe through 1949 to document post-war life in Europe. When he returned to the States, Tony became a photo journalist for *Life* and *Look* magazine, photographing famous figures including John F. Kennedy, Frank Lloyd Wright, and Sophia Loren. Throughout his career, "White Death: Photo Requiem for a Dead Soldier, Private Henry I. Tannenbaum" circled the world through multiple exhibits and books and had become the iconic image of the Battle of the Bulge.

Schiltz also found out that Tony was alive and living in New York City. In 1997, the orphan and the photographer met for the first time.

Tony gave Sam a professional print of the photograph. Tony's greatest joy besides meeting Sam and his family was taking a picture of Henry's grave in Mount Hebron Cemetery, New York City. For Tony, that picture brought him closure after more than fifty years.

In 2002, Sam and Rachel Tannenbaum and Tony Vaccaro flew to Europe as guests of the grateful citizens of Luxembourg and Belgium. The Tannenbaums met with the countries' war orphans. They visited the Henri-Chapelle American Cemetery where Henry was originally buried. In Ottre, Belgium, Sam and Tony placed a wreath at the AWON monument, dedicated to "PVT Henry Irving Tannenbaum and other members of the 83rd Infantry Division." For Sam, it was a "trip of a lifetime."

Fifty-seven years after the then-amateur photographer shot "White Death," Sam Tannenbaum and Tony Vaccaro visited a beautiful tree-filled spot in Ottre, Belgium. The former battle field is now a Christmas tree farm called *Salm Sapin* in French. And in German? Thanks to the famous German folk song now identified with Christmas, it would be associated by many with "O Tannenbaum."

Sam's home in Kissimmee, Florida, is filled with artifacts from his family's history—pictures, books, his father's medals, and a replica of the bracelet Henry was wearing before it was stolen by the German soldiers. "I may not have had the opportunity to tell my parents that I love them," said Sam. "Through telling their story, I believe I am honoring them. And that is, after all, what the Fifth Commandment tells us to do."

The Jewish World, November 9, 2017

Onto My Next Adventure

Now that Larry and I have become summer "residents" of Colorado, I have challenged myself physically more than any earlier time in my life. It is my Rocky Mountain boot camp. I return home thinner, stronger, healthier—and already thinking of our next adventures in the Colorado Rockies.

Our daughter Julie came out to Eagle County, Colorado, in 2003 for a one-year teaching position at an environment school. Fresh out of college, she fell in love with Colorado, the Rockies, and Sam—not necessarily in that order. Fourteen years later, she, Sam, their daughter Sylvie and their dog Neva live in Frisco, Colorado, seventy miles from Denver on the western slope of the Continental Divide.

Until 2015, we would come out to visit them every year for a couple of weeks. Since our granddaughter arrived, we rent a condo close to their home for a couple of months to escape the Florida heat and enjoy being Zayde and Gammy.

As Frisco is located 9100 feet above sea level, Larry and I take a couple of days to acclimate to the altitude. Once we have our mountain lungs, we take advantage of all the area has to offer.

Larry plays in a pickleball league three or four times a week—their motto is "We play with an altitude." On those days, I leave our condo, pick up my granddog Neva, and we take the trail up to Rainbow Lake. It's an easy one-mile hike, only made a little tricky by its popularity. Neva and I have had to share the shoreline with up to twenty people and almost as many dogs. On quieter days, we have the lake to ourselves. We play Neva's version of fetch: I toss a stick into the freezing water; she fetches it; I chase her down to retrieve it. Then we head around the lake, making our way back home along a rushing creek.

When Sam and Julie took us on hikes the initial years we visited, I was intimidated by their longer excursions. Would we get lost? Could I handle the steep climbs? Would I fall off a narrow precipice, my body found by the rescue team a week later? Would we run into a moose or bear? After many years of hiking, my moments of terror are limited only to a few dicey paths that are a little too narrow or steep for my taste. "I'm scared," I utter under my breath.

One of our favorite hikes, Lilypad Lake, takes us along a steep path to a sturdy wooden bridge that spans a rushing creek. Climbing up the stream, we come to a section that overlooks Frisco and Lake Dillon. Another thirty-minute climb through forest paths and wildflowers brings us to a lake on the left and a pond filled with lily pads on the right. As chipmunks beg for crumbs, we enjoy water and a trail bar before heading back down.

The longest, most difficult hike we took this summer was to McCullough Gulch, south of Breckinridge. The entire trip is in the shadow of Quandary Peak, one of Colorado's fifty-three mountain peaks that have an elevation of at least 14,000 feet. A few miles drive up a dirt road took us to a parking lot and a half-mile hike to the trail head. The path up the trail got steeper, muddier, and—in my wimpy opinion—less passable. At one point, a short section of small boulders required some scrambling. Above us, two mountain goats grazed. About one and a half miles up, we made our way to White Falls, a waterfall that cascaded from the lake above us. The sky, up to that point blue with fluffy clouds, got darker. From the waterfall, we made our way to the glacial lake above us.

While not difficult to follow, the path got steeper and required our scrambling around slippery rocks. At one point, we got slightly off trail and needed to climb over some boulders. "I'm scared!" I whispered loudly. Although we were never in any imminent danger of falling, I was saying prayers for our safety. I tried not to think of what our children would say if the broken body of their sixty-something mother was found at the bottom of my imagined crevice. Just as we got to the top of the boulders, a young boy bounded past me to meet the rest of his family on the trail. Pretty embarrassing for me to be so afraid when a child regarded it as standard playground fare.

After climbing a final steep grade, Larry and I reached the beautiful glacial lake at the top of McCullough Gulch. Beyond the lake was the magnificent site of Pacific Peak, a 13,900 footer. We had made it! We ate our snacks, drank some water, and enjoyed the spectacular view.

Tikkun Olam

Although the wind was strong, the sun was shining, and the clouds were fluffy when all of that suddenly changed.

Hail! The skies opened up, and we were pummeled with pea-sized pellets. We put on our raincoats and slipped our way down the mountain, this time avoiding the "rock climb." By the time we got to the waterfall, the hail had turned to spitting rain. A mile further down, the sun came out. Four and a half hours after we started, we had completed the hike, tired but glad we had done it.

Larry and I completed a number of hikes during our eight weeks in Frisco, each one providing breathtaking views of mountains, lakes, waterfalls, and wildflowers. We experienced heat and rain and thunder and lightning and occasional bug swarms, but only once did we have to cut our hike short.

Our last weekend in Colorado, Sam, Larry, Sylvie, Neva and I hiked Black Powder Trail on Boreas Pass. Our two-year-old granddaughter soon tired of riding in her carrier on Sam's back and decided to tackle the steep path on foot. This worked until Sylvie and Neva found a pile of dirt created by burrowing animals that they regarded as more fun than further climbing. After a half hour of digging and snacks, all twenty-two pounds of her led us the way down the trail.

When I share my pictures on Facebook with friends and family, many comment on how strong and brave and fit we had proven ourselves to be. When I share descriptions of our hikes with native Coloradans, however, they are less impressed. "Oh yes! We did that hike in the winter with our snow shoes," they comment. Or "If you enjoyed McCullough Gulch, you should try the thirteen-mile hike up Meadow Lake Trail." I can see clearly why *GetFitTogether.com* has named Colorado the most fit state in the country. And I know already that my granddaughter and I will fit right in.

The Jewish World, August 31, 2017

How I Came to Write a Book

"It was a dark and stormy night. Suddenly shots rang out!" Poor Snoopy! For all his "dogged" attempts, Charles Schultz's beloved beagle has not yet published his novel. Thanks to *The Jewish World*, however, I have been more successful. I have published a book.

Actually, it was a bright and sunny day in June 2013, when Josie Kivort, Hadassah Capital District's Chapter Campaign Chair, and I paid a visit to *The Jewish World's* office. For the past several months, we were serving on the committee to plan the organization's annual Special Gifts event. Jim Clevenson, the publisher of the Schenectady-based biweekly, Josie, and I met to discuss the timeline future press releases and advertisements.

I had communicated with *The Jewish World* mostly through press releases. For years, I had worked on publicity, initially as a volunteer for several organizations in Clifton Park and later in my role as the public relations contact for the Capital District Educational Opportunity Center in Troy. We had been in "virtual contact" as I had been sending the newspaper articles that I viewed as relevant to the Jewish community.

During our discussion, I mentioned to Jim that I had retired three years earlier. Jim asked if I would be interested in doing reporting for the newspaper

"I have done enough press releases for a lifetime," I told Jim. "However, would you be interested in publishing some short non-fiction pieces about my life as a Jewish woman, wife, and mother in Upstate New York?"

Jim agreed to give the idea a try. He told me that I should send the articles to Laurie Clevenson, his sister and the paper's editor-in-chief.

On August 27, 2013, *The Jewish World* published "There Goes My Heart" in its school opening issue. My article recalled how saying goodbye to my children—whether putting them on the bus the first day of kindergarten or dropping off at their dorms their first day of college or waving them off as they got in their own cars and drove across the country to new jobs—always brought me to tears.

I had asked my mother if the farewells ever got easier. "Oh, Marilyn," she said. "Every time any one of you gets into the car and drives away, I think to myself, 'There goes my heart!'"

So started my regular contributions to *The Jewish World*. Every two weeks, I wrote a story and submitted it for the newspaper's consideration. Growing up as the only Jewish family in a small Upstate New York town; experiencing anti-Semitism as an inexperienced high school English teacher; participating in a playgroup for our two-year-olds; adjusting to retirement; leaving the home we shared for thirty-six years to move to Florida—these many once-private moments became very public columns.

Initially, I was afraid I would run out of ideas. As the months progressed, however, I found that even the smallest event— biking up a steep mountain in the Rockies, visiting the Portland Holocaust Memorial, changing my granddaughter's diaper—could morph from an idea to a story. Family and friends shared their experiences, and, with their permission, wove them into my articles.

Not that the stories always flowed easily from my brain to the Mac laptop. "Writing is easy," wrote sports writer Red Smith. "All you do is stare at a blank sheet of paper until drops of blood form on your forehead." I often found myself up at midnight before a deadline trying to polish what I had written. But, like some people I knew who devoted hours to quilting or photography or golf, I devoted hours to my writing.

When I moved to Florida in 2015, I joined SOL Writers, a group of women who met twice a month to share their drafts or to participate in a free write. A few of the women were published authors; others, like me, had dreams of expanding their audience. I brought in pieces I had either completed or were working on for *The Jewish World*. The women were not afraid to criticize but were also generous in their praise. "You seriously need to think about putting these essays into a book," one of my writer friends suggested.

In March 2016, I got up enough courage to contact Mia Crews, a professional editor who would be responsible for formatting the manuscript, designing the cover, and uploading the finished product to Amazon.

Nothing prepared me for the amount of work required to go from a collection of stories to a polished book. I started editing. And editing. And editing. I thought I was close to finishing before we left for our summer trip out west. However, I worked on it on the plane to San Francisco, at nights in different hotels up the Oregon Coast, and during every spare minute during our six-week stay in Colorado. I enlisted Larry's help. The two of us sat together on the couch in our rented condo going over the manuscript with a fine-tooth comb while two political conventions and the Summer Olympics played on the television.

When we got back to Florida, Mia and I completed the final revisions. On September 3, 2016, my sixty-sixth birthday, *There Goes My Heart* was launched on Amazon. I had done it! I had written a real, live book with, as a friend commented, with a cover and pages and nouns and verbs and everything!

"A writer only starts a book," wrote Samuel Johnson. "A reader finishes it." Thanks to Laurie and Jim Clevenson for giving me the opportunity to publish my articles. Thanks to you, my readers, who have helped me reach the finish line of my lifelong dream.

The Jewish World, September 15, 2016

Acknowledgements

Thank you to all my family and friends who told me their stories and gave me permission to share them with my readers.

Thank you to Laurie and Jim Clevenson of the Capital District of New York's *The Jewish World* for publishing many of the stories in this book.

Thank you to Christine Desousa and the *Heritage Florida Jewish News* for publishing recent stories in this book.

Thank you to SOL Writers for encouraging me to publish my articles and books.

Thank you to all my friends and family who offered suggestions on how to improve my writing.

Thank you for the efforts of Mia Crews for bringing this project to life.

Thank you to my parents, Fran and Bill Cohen, who were always there for me.

Thank you to my children, Adam, Julie, and Sam, who give me so much joy.

Thank you to my granddaughter Sylvie, who lights up all our lives.

And a special thank you to Larry Shapiro, my husband, my soulmate, my best friend, my muse, and the subject of (too!) many of my articles!

About the Author

Marilyn Cohen Shapiro grew up in a very close-knit family in a small town on Lake Champlain in upstate New York. Since retiring from a career in adult education and relocating to Florida, she has been writing stories about her family as well as the many interesting people she has had the honor to know. She and her husband Larry have two children, a granddaughter, and a granddog.

Marilyn has been a regular contributor to the bi-weekly publication, *The Jewish World* (Capital Region, NY), since 2013. She also has contributed articles to the (Schenectady, NY) *Gazette* and (Orlando) *Heritage Florida Jewish News*, as well as academic publications. Her first book, *There Goes My Heart*, was published in 2016. Many of her stories are on her blog at *https://theregoesmyheart.me*.

Learn more about the author at www.marilynshapiro.com.
You may email her at *shapcomp18@gmail.com*.

Made in the USA
Columbia, SC
19 November 2020